NOBODY WANTED LAWRENCE WELK— EXCEPT ALL AMERICA!

Incredibly, Lawrence Welk was fired. The powers-that-be in big-time TV had decided he was too old-fashioned for the new generation of hard-rock hippies and swinging singles.

That might have been the end of the Lawrence Welk story. Instead, it was just an incredible new beginning. Because Lawrence Welk and his Musical Family thought they still knew what America wanted. And so, as it turned out, did America.

Now for the first time Lawrence Welk tells the full amazing story of his "comeback"—the comeback of a man and an orchestra that had never been away from the place they wanted most to be, the hearts of their millions and millions of fans.

Perhaps he will make you choke up a bit in spots. Certainly he will have you chuckling a lot in others. And he is guaranteed to make your heart beat just a little faster, your spirits bubble brighter, and your faith in people grow a great deal stronger. Here is Lawrence Welk, working that old Welk magic, giving us all his best— with love.

AH-ONE,

AH-TWO!

"A BOOK THAT LEAVES YOU FEELING ALL'S WELL WITH THE WORLD . . . the heartwarming story of a man who believes in himself and the many people who work with him"
—*Fort Wayne Journal Gazette*

"AH-ONE, AH-TWO! Is filled with behind the scenes portrayals of the special love, devotion and camaraderie between Lawrence Welk and his Musical Family. All of the favorites are here: Champagne Lady; Norma Zimmer; Cissy and Bobby; Guy and Raina; Sandi and Salli; all the singers, dancers, musicians, and of course, the Hotsy Totsy boys . . . Here is a heartwarming success story that features all the drama, humor and excitement that have made Lawrence Welk and his Musical Family household words"
—*Vallejo Times-Herald*

"Lawrence Welk lifts his baton in a crescendo of delight . . . It's a joy to have a book that shares the spirit, love and devotion of his Musical Family. If you are not yet a fan of Lawrence Welk, you will be by the time you've finished AH-ONE, AH-TWO! THANK YOU, MR. WELK—INDEED YOU ARE WUNNERFUL!"
—*The News-Chief*

Also by Lawrence Welk with Bernice McGeehan:

WUNNERFUL, WUNNERFUL!

Ah-One, Ah-Two!

Life with My Musical Family

Lawrence Welk

with Bernice McGeehan

BALLANTINE BOOKS • NEW YORK

Copyright © 1974 by Lawrence Welk

Library of Congress Catalog Card Number: 74-8086

SBN 345-24576-8-175

This edition published by arangement with
Prentice-Hall, Inc.

First Printing: November, 1975

Printed in the United States of America

BALLANTINE BOOKS
A Division of Random House, Inc.
201 East 50th Street, New York, N.Y. 10022
Simultaneously published by
Ballantine Books, Ltd., Toronto, Canada

This book is about my Musical Family. When the thought first came to me to do a book about our orchestra and how it operates, I decided to tell the whole story, the bad as well as the good; to take you backstage and let you see exactly the kind of people we are. In my first book, *Wunnerful, Wunnerful!* I talked about my own life. This second book is about the people who make up the "family" which has become such a big part of my life.

When I finished the book, however, I was a little worried that maybe I had talked too much! But I spoke with various members of our group, and every one of them gave me his blessing and allowed me to go ahead with it, even though I had revealed many of the trouble spots and heartaches which have plagued us over the years. You will find, as you read this, that we are not perfect human beings who never make mistakes. We are human, just as you are, and we falter and fall time and again.

But I think you will also find, as I know in my heart, that the folks in our Musical Family are the most talented, loyal, and cooperative to be found any-where. I have only deep gratitude for the wonderful job they have done for me.

I am, of course, an extremely lucky man. I have not only my own wonderful family, my wife, chil-dren, and grandchildren, but also my wonderful Musical Family, and the family of fans and friends who have supported us so loyally over the years.

This book is dedicated to all of you.

CONTENTS

PART ONE

1

A Door Opens

IT'S NEVER EASY to be fired. It's even harder when you're sixty-eight years old, and you know that two hundred other people will lose their jobs if you lose yours. But that's what happened to me one day in March of 1971, and even now, whenever I think about it, I get a kind of sick feeling.

I had been hoping against hope for months, that the American Broadcasting Company would keep our musical show on the air just as they had for the previous sixteen years. I was aware, of course, that a great many other television programs had been canceled during that 1970–71 season, but I hadn't been seriously concerned about ours, at first. For one thing, we had been on the air nationwide, every week for those sixteen years, the only musical show in television to make that kind of record. Also, we had a large and very loyal audience, our ratings had held up consistently, and I knew that our sponsors were happy with us. So it didn't seem reasonable to me that ABC would cancel us.

But when they failed to renew their option early in March as they always had before, I felt a real stab of worry, and I dispatched my manager-agents, Don Fedderson and Sam Lutz, to New York to find out exactly where we stood. When they returned, they didn't know a whole lot more than they had when they left.

"The thing is, Lawrence," said Don, running a hand through his thick sand-colored hair, "everything is in a turmoil right now. The Federal Communications

Directive has everybody all fired up, and also—ABC has committed itself totally to the youth wave." He paused. "But you're still very much in the running, and Elton told me they wouldn't make any decision for a few more weeks yet." Elton was Elton Rule, president of ABC, and a man with whom we had always enjoyed a fine relationship.

I was both encouraged and dismayed at his report. I knew that the Federal Communications Directive to which he referred, had ordered the three major networks to return a half-hour of prime time to local stations, hoping that this would stimulate more creativity on their part, and lessen the power of the networks. In theory I was in complete agreement with this idea. But the directive had seemed to throw the networks into a panic, and they had been lopping off long-established shows right and left. In addition, there was a growing reliance, at that time, on the science of "demographics"—breaking down a viewing audience as to its age, sex, and economic status. The trend then, was to aim more and more shows toward the teen-age audience in the belief that they were the ones who bought the most advertised products . . . or else their parents bought the products for them! As a result, network heads began developing programs which appealed to a very young audience instead of those appealing to other age groups.

I knew all this and it was a little disturbing, particularly since we were known as a show which had a great many mothers and fathers among the viewers. But I had always felt that we had more of a "family" audience than anything else, one which included people of all ages. Also, a survey of our own indicated that we were beginning to attract more and more young people every week ourselves. So I managed to stay hopeful.

But as the days went by, and the phone call from ABC telling us we had been renewed for another year didn't come through, the suspense became almost unbearable, and I ached to do something about it. "I just know if I flew back to New York and talked to the ABC management myself I could sell the show," I told Don. "I know it!"

Don turned pale at the very idea. "No, no, you can't do that!" he said vehemently. "Stars can't do that! That's what agents are for. That's my job— Sam's!"

"I'm not a star. I'm just a man with a wonderful group of people and a show we love to do and I want to save it for all of us. Please, Don, let me go."

But Don was adamant and so was Sam. I think they would have held on to my coattails if I had tried to go and so, reluctantly, I gave in. But I could hardly stand not knowing what was happening and I kept in close daily communication with Don and Sam. That is to say, I drove them crazy trying to find out what was going on. "I just this minute talked to New York," Don would say patiently. "They haven't made a decision yet. The minute they do I'll call you."

At one point he called to tell me ABC had whittled the list of prospective shows down to twelve, from which they would finally choose six. I took a look at that list and I didn't see how we could miss! I confidently expected the phone to ring any minute and tell us we were in.

But it didn't. And for the next few days the tension continued to build until we could hardly stand it.

Somewhere in the middle of it all I celebrated my sixty-eighth birthday, although "celebrate" is not, perhaps, the right word! I asked my family to forego the usual party. Instead, I opened hundreds of beautiful birthday cards in my den at home, and worked on a magazine article until late that night. But I couldn't concentrate, and every time the phone rang my heart skipped a beat.

Finally on Monday, March 15, Don did receive a call from ABC in New York, asking for one week's option on the show and indicating that they would reach a decision "momentarily." We were jubilant and our spirits shot right up to the skies. Next day, however, they plunged right down again when we read an item in one of the trade papers that the show had been canceled. My secretary, Lois Lamont, burst into tears when she read it, but almost before I had a chance to offer her my hankie we received an apologetic phone call assuring us that report had been false. (And the combined sigh of relief from everyone in the office nearly blew the offending newspaper right off the desk.)

Wednesday and Thursday dragged by somehow. I played golf both days, trying to work out some of my excess energy and frustration, and on Thursday night my wife, Fern, and I went to a dinner party. I had picked up the worst cold I've ever had in my life by then, and I would have welcomed a chance to stay in bed the next day. But I had already agreed to play in a week-end golf tournament in Escondido, my mobile homes resort about forty miles north of San Diego, so very early on Friday, March 19, my business manager, Ted Lennon, and I made the trip down. I got in the back seat of my car, rolled up in a blanket and tried to nap as Ted drove through the early morning fog along the Coast Highway. But between wiping my eyes, blowing my nose, and trying not to think about what was happening, sleep was impossible. I gave up and climbed back in the front seat.

Once out on the golf course I felt better. The fresh air and total concentration which golf demands always helps me forget my troubles. But on the fourteenth hole . . . which I played at par as I recall . . . I came back to reality with a rush. A messenger was waiting there, anxious to drive me back to the motel immediately, for a "very important long-distance phone call from New York."

This was it then. The call for which we'd all been waiting. I was filled with wild impatience as we sped back to the motel and, as we neared the office, an almost overpowering surge of hope and elation. Surely . . . surely if they were bringing me in off the golf course in order to talk to me . . . then the news must be very good!

But it wasn't, of course. And for just a moment, on that cool and gray afternoon, that phone call ended my world completely.

I sat where I was, in the motel office, unable to move, almost unable to talk. The call hadn't been from ABC as I'd expected. It had been from a reporter in New York who asked me almost casually how I felt about the fact that our show had just been canceled. "ABC has just released its official list of shows for the new fall season," he said, "and you're not on the list. How do you feel about that, Mr. Welk?"

For a second or two I really couldn't answer him, but somehow I dredged up enough strength to say I felt far worse for my musical family than I did for myself. I added that I hoped we could find some way to stay on the air and, even to me, my voice sounded quite calm and steady. But my hands shook when I tried to hang up the phone, and I couldn't have moved even if I wanted to. Seconds before, I had been a man with a forty-five piece musical group, an orchestra, and a show that had been on television for twenty consecutive years, sixteen of them nationwide. Now, I had nothing—no show, no contracts, no firm future to offer my musical family, nothing. I felt just about as bad as a man can feel. In fact, when I first heard those words from the reporter, I died a little. There is no other way to describe it.

After a while I got up stiffly, like an old man, and

went quietly out the back way and down the hill toward my mobile home. The evening shadows were beginning to lengthen, and I was grateful for them. I wanted to slip away and hide for a while, be alone and think this thing through.

At the house I called the switchboard and asked them to hold my calls. I knew I would have to face inquiries from other reporters before long, and I tried to steel myself and compose little speeches. But I couldn't. I had made myself believe so thoroughly that we wouldn't lose, couldn't lose, that I really hadn't thought about what to say if we were canceled. Now, I found, I couldn't.

It got completely dark outside, with just a little light filtering in through the dining-room windows overlooking the golf course. I sat down at the table and tried to think clearly.

But I was dazed. And suddenly time itself slipped away and I felt almost as I had forty years earlier, on the night my entire band had walked out on me in Dallas, South Dakota. That time, too, I had felt numb and sick. The fellows had made it very plain that they were leaving because they believed I would never make it in the music business and I was the one who was holding them all back. I had felt ashamed, almost destroyed by what they did that night. And yet, I thought with a sudden spurt of hope—I *had* been able to make it! Only then, I had been in my twenties. Now, I was close to seventy.

I got up and began to pace the floor restlessly. What should I do? What *could* I do? I could retire, I thought rather ironically, and Fern and our daughters, Shirley and Donna, had been urging me to do so for a long time. But some of the men in my band had been with me twenty-five years or more; they were as close to me as brothers. And some of the youngsters in the group, just starting out, were as dear to me as if they were my own. I couldn't just walk out and leave them.

I wondered if our fans would be upset, if we would get any reaction from them. I wondered wretchedly if my good friend and sponsor, Matty Rosenhaus, would be disappointed in us, would feel that we had somehow let him down. And I wondered wearily what would have happened if we had done things differently, worked a little harder, tried different formats. They were all hard questions—and there were no easy answers.

There were times, during that black hour, when the thought of retiring became more and more attractive to me. Financially I was well able to do so, and retirement would mean an end to all the worries and pressures like the ones facing me now. I would have time to play golf and read the books that meant so much to me, time to be with my family. But, no matter what direction my thoughts went, they kept coming back to one central and overriding theme—my concern for the members of my Musical Family, my "kids." And I know, sitting there in the dark, that I could never let them down. I'd try my best to keep things going so they would have some kind of security, and I'd act confident and cheerful if it killed me! It might not help us stay in business, but it would certainly help our morale.

I was almost surprised at how bad I felt. I had always thought that the worst time in my life had been that night in Dallas when my whole band had rejected me. But I realized, sitting there alone in the dark, that something far worse had happened. Because then, I had had just Fern and myself to think about. Now, I had a whole "family."

I don't know how long I sat there. Maybe half an hour, maybe only five minutes, but eventually I began to get control of myself. I got up, turned on a few lights so the place didn't look quite so much like a funeral parlor, switched on the stereo for the music that always revives me, and went in to take a shower. I had already invited sixteen friends for dinner that night, and, canceled show or not, I would keep that date. In the shower I could hear the bedside phone beginning to ring, and by the time I was out and toweling dry, it began to ring without stopping. I pulled on my robe and began to take the calls. First Don, sick at heart when he discovered I had already been told the news so baldly. He himself had just been notified by ABC and he'd been calling me every ten minutes, hoping to beat the reporters. I assured him I was fine, and then I talked with Sam, and then Fern who said loyally, "Lawrence, please don't feel bad if your bubble machine has broken down! You've proved your point and you've earned a rest." Just hearing from her made me feel better, and by the time I was dressed and on my way to the restaurant, my spirits were beginning to rise. And when I walked into the dining room and was met by a burst of warm and friendly applause from the guests, I felt even better . . . applause always stimulates me!

Talking about the whole thing helped, too, and I discovered I could even joke about it. "Well, you know it isn't so much that I mind getting fired," I told everybody, "but did they have to pull me off the golf course to tell me about it! Now that's just *too* much!"

We had no sooner sat down for dinner than the waitress came up to tell me that I had another "very important" long-distance call. After the one I'd just received, I wasn't any too anxious to take another! "Ask them if I can call back, will you please?" I said. "We're just starting to eat."

She nodded and went away but a moment later she was back again, looking a little harassed. "I'm sorry, Mr. Welk," she whispered, "but they insist on talking to you. They say it's most important."

"Very well." I put down my napkin, excused myself and went into the foyer to take the call, mentally composing a cheerful little speech for the reporter. But it was not a reporter. It was my sponsor, Matty Rosenhaus, and if I live to be a hundred, I'll never forget what he said. "Lawrence?" His voice was warm with concern and the words came quickly. "Lawrence, we just heard the bad news. Now listen—don't worry! You'll be right back on top again, I know it! And no matter what direction you take to get there—well . . . we want to go along with you." He paused and then added simply, "Lawrence—I believe in you."

It's funny how your world can go full circle in just a few hours. At four o'clock that afternoon I had been crushed, just sickened that the hopes and dreams and accomplishments of twenty years could have been wiped out so quickly, almost casually. I had been half convinced that our professional life was over. Yet here I was at seven o'clock feeling as if I'd been given a new lease on life! I practically ran back to our table, where I tapped on a water glass for everyone's attention, and then, looking at that circle of dear and familiar faces, I said . . . "Friends . . . something almost unbelievable has just happened! That call was from Matty Rosenhaus. And he said . . ." To my horror I could feel my voice beginning to thicken, so I stopped and cleared my throat and tried again. "He said that no matter what direction we decided to go with the band . . . he would like to go along with us. And Matty said that he . . . that he . . . still believes in me." I'm afraid the tears did come then, but they were tears of joy, releasing all the pain and anguish and worry of the past harrowing weeks. I got busy explaining to everyone that I was wiping my eyes because I had such a terrible cold but I don't think anyone was too fooled. Most of them were in tears themselves as they began crowding around, congratulating me, shaking my hand. Bert and Nancy Carter, who had been instrumental in getting me in television in the first place, were the first to rush up, and little Nancy, who is barely five feet tall, flung her arms around me and hugged me tightly. "Oh, Lawrence," she whispered, fiercely, tears shining in her eyes, "that's just wonderful! Wonderful! You're not down yet!"

I hugged her back. No, we weren't down yet, not by a long shot. We had a long way to go, true, and at the moment I had no clear idea as to just which way we'd be going. I only knew that, with Matty's faith and confidence in us—we were on our way again.

2
The Lawrence Welk Network

THE NEXT MORNING, very early, I was up and on the phone with Don and Sam in Los Angeles, talking about the possibilities open to us. I suggested doing three or four television "specials" a year, combined with an extension series of cross-country tours. "That ought to keep the kids busy." Don brought up the idea of producing our own show and releasing it on syndication, but that seemed like a very complex and costly venture, and one that offered no guarantee of success. And we discussed another longheld dream of mine, taking the entire company around the world on tour. We began to come up with so many ideas that finally Don said, "Now, look, what we have to do is decide which of these options is best for us and then concentrate on that!" All of us agreed . . . but none of us could decide which one was best! As it turned out, we didn't have to make a decision. It was made for us. That Saturday saw the beginning of our own special miracle.

All day long the telephone calls came in, not only at Escondido, but all across the nation. Television stations and newspaper offices everywhere began to receive a tremendous number of calls from fans who had just learned about our cancellation and were protesting it. The calls were sporadic to start with, but they marked the beginning of what some observers have called the greatest outpouring of telephone calls in the history of television. We learned later that the ABC outlet, in Hollywood alone, had received more than seven thousand calls the first weekend, and had finally been forced to put on a special switchboard operator just to handle the "Welk" calls. Some of the fans were so outraged they called other networks by mistake, and at least one harried NBC official protested wearily. "Madam, please, *I* didn't have anything to do with Mr. Welk's cancellation!"

The telephone calls continued to come in without letup and by Wednesday we were all aware that something really fantastic was happening, because the mail began to pour in in unprecedented waves too . . . cards, letters, petitions, telegrams, hundreds of thousands of them, sent in by people who were incensed on our behalf and wanted to do something about it. The mail inundated not only our offices, but also ABC, and TV stations and newspaper offices in every part of the country. It was as if somebody, somewhere, had given a giant signal and people everywhere had responded. But the wonderful, magical thing about this outpouring of affection was that it was completely spontaneous. It was a grass-roots kind of demonstration that arose out of a compulsion to do something as an individual, and in a way it was a powerful demonstration of what the average American can do when he wants to. Our letter writers didn't have a huge corporation or any kind of massive centralized direction behind them. They were simply individual Americans determined to do as much as they could, to keep a show they had grown to enjoy, on the air, and they were resorting to the strongest weapon of all. They were exercising the power of their individual choice.

They made their wishes known in a variety of colorful ways, too! Some of the letters came in on lined school paper, others on the finest engraved stationery. Some of them were actually lengthy petitions, signed by as many as three hundred people, with the "petition" part inscribed on parchment paper decorated with champagne bubbles or flowers or musical notes. One group of determined fans near Tuscaloosa, Alabama, took up a collection and rented space on a billboard demanding that we be returned. Churches put up notices on their bulletin boards. Our wonderful fans not only wrote us and the network, they also wrote to our sponsors, and they bombarded TV entertainment editors from coast to coast! One editor wrote a column I saved because it was so hilarious. In it he wrote that he had ventured to criticize our show and had nearly been smothered in an avalanche of letters the following week. "Never," quoth he, "underestimate the power of a little old lady wearing tennis shoes and carrying a Welk record!" But it wasn't only little old ladies who wrote to us. The mothers are, and always will be, the heart and soul of our audience, but we also got a great deal of mail from men and women in the over-forty age bracket, plus a tremendous number of children and a surprising amount from young adults. They wrote us the most wonderful, warm, encouraging letters you can imagine. All of them stick in my mind, and one of them I can recite word for word. "Dear Mr. Welk," it read. "Every Saturday night for the past sixteen years my wife and I have had a date with you. She sets up the card table in our living room with candles and flowers, and we eat our dinner there and pretend we are at the Palladium Ballroom in Hollywood. We are not young anymore, but every time your orchestra plays a dance tune, I invite her to dance. Please, please—don't take our Saturday night "date" away from us."

I loved those letters, and I knew from the coverage we were getting in the papers that we were receiving an unusual number of them. Even so, I didn't realize the full extent of the mail until almost two weeks after our cancellation. That morning I walked into our

offices to find Julie Jobe, my pretty receptionist, looking just as pretty as usual, but also a trifle strained.
That wasn't like Julie at all, and when I walked on
down the hall to Lois' office and found her looking
rather glum, too, I knew something was up. "What's
the matter?" I inquired.

"Take a look in the mail room," said Lois shortly.
"Go ahead. Just take a look!"

I opened the door and took a look, and I was
flabbergasted at what I saw. There were stacks of
mail, piles of it. Cards and letters of every description
were jammed into cardboard cartons which took up
every available square inch of space in the room.
There were cartons piled on top of desks, tables,
filing cabinets, chairs, and even some on top of the
watercooler in the corner. I could see more boxes
stacked almost to the ceiling in the corridor outside.
Margaret Heron, our mail clerk, and Laurie Rector,
our assistant office manager, sat sniffling drearily in
the midst of this mountain of mail, and when Laurie
saw me she burst into tears. "Oh, we'll never get
all this mail answered!" she sobbed. "Never!" A couple
of the others were also dabbing their eyes and sniffling
surreptitiously in the corner. In fact, I've never seen
our girls so low.

I cleared my throat. "Uh . . . now girls," I said,
"C'mon, dry those tears, and we'll have some coffee.
Come on, follow me!"

We went down to our employees' lounge at the
end of our suite of offices, and I began boiling water.
"Laurie, get the tea bags," I ordered. "Barbara,
where's the sugar? And somebody get the coffee."

Presently we were all relaxing, laughing a little,
and I said, "Girls . . . I know how upset you are
. . . but think how awful it would be if we didn't
get any mail at all. Then you really would have something to cry about!"

"Oh, it's not that," said Laurie. "We're not complaining about how much mail we get, believe me! It's just that we don't see how you can ever answer all of those letters."

"Well," I said after a moment, "I'm sure we can do it. It may take a little longer than usual, but—we can do it."

"Oh, Lawrence," said Laurie despairingly, "there must be at least a hundred thousand letters in there!"

Laurie was mistaken. There weren't a hundred thousand letters. There were closer to a million. When we totaled up the entire count months later, we discovered that we had received over one million pieces of mail! To this day I am staggered at the thought that more than a million people took the time and trouble to write. And I truly believe that it was those letters—combined with the phone calls—that made the difference for us. All those people standing up and demanding to be counted are what kept our show on the air.

Laurie was right about one thing, however. There simply wasn't enough time to answer all the mail personally, and send out a Christmas greeting, too, as we had always done. So we compromised and sent a Christmas letter instead, explaining what had happened.

Don was electrified by the enormity of the response.

"Well, that's it, Lawrence," he said simply, gesturing at the stack of mail. "There's your answer! You've got an audience ready and waiting to see you on syndication!"

"Yes, but—what about the independent TV stations?" I asked doubtfully. "We don't know if they want us."

"No, we don't. But we can find out soon enough! And if we can line up enough stations to carry the show, then I think that without question we should produce it on our own and market it ourselves. Why,

Lawrence—" his face was glowing—"you could build
your own television network!"

The thought was almost overwhelming, but even
so I was inclined to go along with his advice. For
one thing, I knew he was not alone in his thinking.
My producer, Jim Hobson, and musical director,
George Cates, as well as Sam, had already said much
the same thing, and so had my good friend Ed Kletter,
president of the Parkson Advertising Agency in New
York which had long represented Matty Rosenhaus'
interests. In fact, he had told Don that his research
indicated we would pull about seven million families
to start with on syndication, and that he and Matty
could go along comfortably with that figure. "And
if I know Lawrence," he added, "he'll build that up
to at least as big an audience as he ever had on ABC,
and probably bigger!" The confidence of these men
was a great influence on my thinking, and so was
the unbelievable support of our fans. But there was
something else, too. My "kids." They had demon-
strated a kind of loyalty and love during these past
few difficult days beyond anything I had any right
to expect. Every one of them expressed their goodwill
(Norma Zimmer had been the first to call) and every
one had said virtually the same thing: "Please let
me help, Lawrence. I want to do whatever I can."
So I knew that if we tried to establish our own syndicated series, they would be with me every inch of
the way . . . and I think that may have been the de-
ciding factor in my thinking. At any rate, after a moment's indecision, I reached across the desk, grabbed
Don's hand and said, "Okay, Don . . . let's try!"

Don swung into action immediately, and when
he's in top form nothing can stop him! He recruited
Jack Minor to help out. Jack, who has blue eyes,
blond hair, and energy to burn, was one of the men
originally responsible for getting me on television

in the first place, and he's never stopped kidding me about it. "I'm always torn between bragging about discovering you," he tells me frequently, "or apologizing for it!" But he stopped kidding when Don asked for help, and plunged in to work right around the clock along with Sam, and by week's end the three men had enough facts and figures on hand to call a strategy meeting at my house at six o'clock in the evening.

We were all very excited that night. I recall that Don strode down the long hallway to our family room, carting a load of books and papers and charts in one hand, gesturing with the other, and talking nonstop all the way. Then he plunked himself down in a leather armchair with his right foot crossed up over his left knee, a sure sign he was ready for action. Ted Lennon, my business manager, was there also, along with Charlie Spiro of the Fedderson office, Jim Hobson, Sam, Jack, and of course Lois, busy with her notebook and pencil.

"This is a rough draft of a telegram we propose sending to every independent TV station in the country," Don said rapidly, as he passed copies around to each of us. "In it we tell them we will produce thirty-two top-quality hour-long television shows, and we'll mail them a tape of the show four weeks in advance so they can run off a duplicate for their own use. And . . ." he turned to me, "it won't cost them a cent."

My head snapped up. "Won't cost them? Why not?"

Don grinned, a little craftily. "We'll give them the show free of charge—but we'll retain a certain amount of national sponsorship time for ourselves. Then we'll give them five minutes of commercial air time for their own use. No money involved at all. It's a new concept, Lawrence, never been done before."

It was my turn to grin. "Don," I said, "you may

think this has never been done before, but I was doing it forty years ago in radio."

"Oh?"

"Yes. When the boys and I were playing for Chan Gurney at WNAX in Yankton, we did one half hour for him free of charge and he advertised his Gurney hog tonic and chicken feed. In return he gave us a free half hour, and we lined up our own sponsors. No money involved there either, and it worked very well."

"Well, it's the same idea exactly," said Don. "So—if you agree, Lawrence—we propose sending these telegrams off right away and see what kind of reception we get."

I took a look at the telegram, which outlined the idea Don had mentioned, and ended: "Please wire if interested and state the hour between seven and ten P.M. any day of week when you can clear time for show."

"We're doing that," explained Don, "so we can get the show set in roughly the same time slot all across the country, probably Saturday or Sunday, just as usual."

"I see." I looked around the room. "Well, this makes good sense to me, gentlemen. What about you?"

There was a general murmur of agreement. "All right. What's the next step?"

"The next step," said Don, looking a little grim, "is to get these telegrams off and wait for the results. We can't do a thing till we know how many stations want to carry the show."

"I think you'll be pleasantly surprised," said Sam. "I know I've had at least a hundred calls from station managers."

"A hundred!" said Don, impressed. "I'm surprised already."

"Well," said Sam, a little sheepishly, "maybe not a hundred. But a lot!"

We all laughed. Sam's enthusiasm sometimes carries him away. "Well, you are gonna be surprised," he insisted. "Wait and see."

That night Don and Jack sent out six hundred telegrams to stations in every part of the country. Within forty-eight hours they had received over four hundred replies, either asking for more information, or else giving a definite order to carry the show! We were delighted at the response, and very touched by some of the answers we received, too. One wire I remember in particular, came in from Ward Quaal of WGN in Chicago and it said, simply—"Yes! We want you back again Lawrence. Pelase come home."

Don began getting up at daybreak in order to talk with station managers back East, and he and Jack worked literally without sleep for the next few days, as they answered the flood of inquiries, and hammered out the beginning links in what we hoped would be our chain of stations.

Meanwhile, Jim Hobson began scouring the town looking for the best people and the best facilities to help produce the show. In the end we managed to keep all the top people who had been with us over the years art director Charles Koon (a "genius" by Jim's description), costume designer Rose Weiss (the best in the business), and our three, long-time . . . and superb . . . cameramen, Jim Angel, Jim Baldin, and Herm Falk. And after checking out other studios, Jim recommended that we stay on at ABC, as they offered us by far the best deal insofar as production costs were concerned. I was very happy to do that. We had worked at ABC for so long it seemed like home anyway, and this meant we could keep working in the same studio with exactly the same facilities we'd always had. Except for one thing. Somehow—in the move from network to syndication—I lost my dressing room!

I didn't know about it till the day I returned from our personal appearance tour the following September. When I went to open my dressing-room door, I found it locked, so I hunted up a maintenance man and explained the situation. For some reason he seemed terribly embarrassed and finally he muttered, "Uh . . . Mr. Welk . . . didn't anybody tell you you have a new dressing room now?"

"No," I said. "I do? Why?"

"Well," he said, "you know . . . Miss Andrews is taping here now."

Then I remembered that ABC had signed Julie Andrews, the lovely English singing star, to do a series. There had been much talk about a lavishly redecorated new dressing room for her, but I hadn't realized until just this minute that it was going to be *my* old dressing room they would lavishly redecorate!

"Well, okay," I said equably. "Where do I dress?"

Vastly relieved, he led me across the stage to a small room which had formerly been used by our girls for quick costume changes. Lois was miffed at the size of our new quarters, but I didn't mind. During my lifetime in the business I've changed clothes out in the cornfields, behind a screen, a bass drum, a tube, or anything else big enough to hide me . . . and I've probably been in the inside of more men's rooms than anybody else in America. So I wasn't the least bit concerned over our new room. "It's okay," I told Lois. "Don't you remember the dressing room I had when I first came here?" She laughed. My lavish quarters then had consisted of one small room off the men's room. As a matter of fact, the fellows had to go *through* my dressing room in order to get to the men's room, and the constant parade didn't do much toward settling my nerves. "This is fine," I told her.

Actually I thought the whole thing was funny, because it was just one more chapter in the long-running saga of Me and My Dressing Rooms at ABC. The first dressing room, as I said, was the small one off the men's room. A little later, however, ABC signed Frank Sinatra to do a season for them, and in a spasm of gratitude for his services, they brought in an oversized trailer which they fitted out with everything imaginable. It was really something. I know, because when Mr. Sinatra departed ABC, I fell heir to the trailer and I thoroughly enjoyed it for the next few seasons. But then along came Jerry Lewis and he signed to do a late-night talk show, and once again the network went to pieces trying to find some way to express their appreciation, and they built him the biggest, most lavish dressing room you can imagine, with enough chairs and sofas to house a small army. But after one season, Mr. Lewis also departed from ABC, and guess who got the nod again. That's right, me! A couple of my friends thought I should make a few demands from ABC. "After all," they said, "you've been starring on the network for years. ABC should build you a special dressing room." I shook my head. "Why should I?" I asked gently. "I'm doing all right this way!"

But the dressing-room facilities were the least of my considerations during those hectic days. Every hour seemed to bring forth another consideration, another decision. In addition to everything else, we had to prepare a new show for our annual appearance at Tahoe, scheduled for June, as well as get ready for our personal appearance tour in August. Both events had been set up for months, long before our cancellation, but now they loomed as more important than ever. All of us worked at a feverish pace, and it seemed to me that I gave out more interviews during those days than I ever have, before or since. Everyone wanted to know how we had reacted to the shock of the cancellation, and what our future plans were. Most of the reporters were encouraging but a few were skeptical. "Why don't you quit while you're ahead?" was a sentence I heard many times, or "Why don't you quit, you don't need the money." Money had nothing to do with it and never had. It was what we had forged together as a team, a Musical Family, that I wanted to save. It was what we all wanted.

One moment my spirits were very high and I'd marvel at how quickly we seemed to be building our new syndicated series. Then, I'd realize we had by the same token obligated ourselves to produce thirty-two brand new, hour-long, expensively mounted television shows at the same time. My stomach would take a sickening plunge! But on the whole, those were some of the most exhilarating days I can recall.

Don and Sam, along with Jack and Irving Ross, who was acting as general manager of "Project Syndication," worked without letup. They hung a map of the United States on the office wall, and as each new station was confirmed, they marked its location with a red pin. The map looked rather spotty to start with . . . "looks like it's got a case of the measles," I complained mildly, but I could see for myself that every day the trail of red dots grew thicker, increasing sometimes by one or two, sometimes by as many as twenty.

The fellows were building up a very strong network, making a point of selecting the best station in each locality, the ones with the widest coverage or finest reputation. In city after city it was the local ABC outlet itself which asked to carry our show first. I must say this gave us all a case of extreme pleasure! In fact, the whole thing gave us great pleasure, the response was so tremendous and so instantaneous.

I knew that things were going very well for us,

but I wasn't sure how close we were to our goal until the day I dropped into the office unexpectedly and found Don standing in front of the map, his head cocked to one side, his horn-rimmed glasses shoved back on his forehead, and a look almost of wonder on his face. When he heard me he turned around, and then he smiled. "Lawrence," he said gently, "come over here and take a look at this. See here? There are two hundred and twelve stations there, completely firmed and ready to go next September! Think of that, Lawrence. That's almost thirty more than you ever had on ABC." He turned back to the map and ran his finger lightly along the tracery of dots running from coast to coast on the map. "For a kid from Strasburg," he said softly, "you did all right. There you are, Lawrence. There's your Lawrence Welk Network."

Don has been with me at many memorable times in my life. He came into my office in 1954 to tell me we had our first coast-to-coast television show. He's brought in ratings and reports over the years that have made all of us very happy. But I think that moment in the office when we looked at the network our fans and friends had helped us build, was one of the nicest of all. It made me think again that no door ever closes without another one opening. And that maybe our cancellation by ABC hadn't been a bad thing after all.

PART TWO

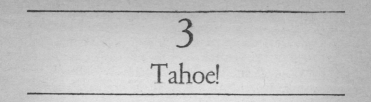

3

Tahoe!

TWO MONTHS LATER we took the first major step on the long road back to our new beginning in television, with our appearance at Harrah's in Lake Tahoe, Nevada. A great many things had happened to us in the meantime. We rehearsed exhaustively for our Tahoe opening. We had completed plans for the extensive personal-appearance tour to follow almost immediately. And, we had taped our last show for ABC. Now, we were truly on our own. The challenge was tremendous.

As usual, I fretted about everything there was to fret about! For one thing, I knew we had to convince at least seven million families to change their viewing habits and switch over to us on our new independent stations. That meant an awesome job of information and publicity, and it was one reason I was so anxious to go on tour it would be a good way to acquaint our fans with our new schedule.

As far as the tour itself went I wasn't really worried at all, because everything was in the hands of Lon Varnell, a Southern gentleman from Nashville, Tennessee, and the best tour manager in the country, a master in the field. And too, I could see from the frequent reports he was sending me that the ticket sales were shaping up very nicely, with several of our dates already sold out. But in the place that meant the most of all—Madison Square Garden in New York City—the sales were lagging badly. I was very disappointed about that. The Garden represented a pinnacle to me. I had long been anxious to play there, because

I felt that a successful appearance in the Garden would give us a tremendous edge as we went into syndication, and might help open the door to a far wider audience. So even though the initial ticket sales were discouragingly slow, I decided to keep it on our schedule. At least for a little while!

Those two things were enough to keep me busy worrying, but there was something else bothering me, too, and that was the fact that we needed at least one more sponsor. Matty Rosenhaus had practically saved our lives and given us the incentive to go ahead, but he couldn't be expected to carry the whole show, and unless we found an additional sponsor to help underwrite the costs, it meant we'd be losing money every week. As tight as I am, that didn't appeal to me at all. I seldom sparkle when I know I'm losing money at the same time! The problem was not so much finding sponsors, as finding the right ones. When I was at ABC, I had it written in my contract that I wouldn't work for any company in whose products I didn't believe myself. Naturally, that limited our selection of sponsors quite a bit. So I was very anxious to get everything settled . . . including my stomach . . . before we left on tour. Don was annoyed when I mentioned this to him "Oh, Lawrence, we have weeks to find the right sponsor!" he said distractedly. "Now don't worry about it!"

And in truth I found it very hard to worry about anything, as Fern and I prepared to fly to Tahoe. There's something about that clear air and sparkling sunshine that makes it a pleasure just to breathe. I could feel my spirits start to rise the moment we landed at nearby Reno, and when I spotted the block-long, chauffeur-driven Rolls-Royce that Bill Harrah always sends to meet us, they rose even further. Fern and I settled down in solitary splendor in the back seat of the car as it began to roll grandly down the highway toward Tahoe. At Carson City we stopped for our yearly ritual purchase . . . one ice cream cone apiece. Then we got back in the car and, surrounded by a profusion of tortoise shell, tufted velvet, stereo music, air conditioning, and little crystal window vases with red roses in them, we contentedly ate our cones. Looking at the silent and dignified chauffeur in the front seat and all the grandeur in the back, I couldn't resist a sidelong wink at Fern. "Well," I stage-whispered, "is this really living or isn't it?"

She grinned. "Not bad for a couple of squares from North Dakota," she acknowledged, licking some ice cream off her fingers.

We went directly to Skyland Manor, the home which Bill Harrah always sets aside for our use. It's built right at the edge of the lake, which is, to my mind, one of the most beautiful places in the world. I've seen the lake when it's sparkling and blue under the summer sun, or churned into black frothy waves in a sudden storm, and either way, it's just beautiful. And the house isn't bad either! Four bedrooms with private balconies, patios, a swimming pool, private stretch of beach, a nice selection of Rolls and Cadillacs in the garage in case we feel like taking a little spin, and our own maid and cook. Even after twelve consecutive years at Tahoe, I never quite got used to all that luxury, and I always feel that one more week will spoil me.

We were scheduled to rehearse all the following day . . . a Tuesday . . . and again on Wednesday, right up till show time, with the opening set for eight-fifteen, and a midnight performance to follow. This was one of the most important bookings we'd ever have. Our whole future depended on it to some degree because this was the show we'd be taking on tour, as well as the one we'd use for the first show of our new television series. A great deal was riding on it, and bright and early the next morning I was at Harrah's, itching to get started.

Most nightclubs look pretty dreary in the daytime, but not Harrah's. The red linen cloths on all the tables are always fresh and crisp, the leather banquettes polished and shining, the red-flowered carpet immaculately clean. I stood on stage for a moment, looking out over the dim, quiet room, savoring the feel of it, the sense of anticipation common to empty theaters everywhere. I picked out a table in the center of the room to direct operations, and just as I did, George Thow, my continuity writer, appeared carrying a briefcase, followed by Lois with her portable typewriter. Jim Hobson, our producer, sauntered in next, looking like a Harvard undergraduate in his cashmere sweater and slacks, and then our musical director, George Cates, burst in. I don't know why I say burst, except that even when he's relaxing, George seems to be in a state of tension!

Meanwhile Bob McClure, Harrah's resident producer, who had earlier flown into Los Angeles to observe our Palladium rehearsals, appeared with his crew and set up a table adjoining ours, and by ten o'clock, Jack Imel reported that the entire cast was present and ready to go.

Everyone wore very casual rehearsal clothes, the girls in slacks and blouses, the fellows in jeans or double-knit pants (although our trumpet player, Johnny Zell, turned up unaccountably wearing shorts and a duck hunter's cap), but we weren't casual about the rehearsal. We were deadly serious. We stopped and started, stopped and started, played parts of a number and then . . . knowing the rest of it had already been sufficiently rehearsed . . . jumped to another segment which needed more. To the uninitiated, the whole scene would probably have held a chaotic quality, and it's true that most rehearsals seem like chaos, but it's organized chaos! Ours really went off quite well, I thought, and by the time we'd finished at five o'clock I felt we'd accomplished a lot.

That night we were guests of Mr. Harrah at Perry Como's closing performance, and Perry was so good I got a bad case of stage fright! "How in the world can we ever follow you?" I asked him despairingly after the show. He just laughed, but really, he was wonderful. He sat on a stool, in a single spotlight, and sang eight songs right in a row, and he sang them with such warmth and simplicity that he held the audience in the palm of his hand. Behind him, the orchestra supported him with a clarity of tone and arrangement that made my heart thump. "Hear that?" I whispered to my kids. "You hear how 'clean' he's singing? *That's* what I mean!" He was doing something I have stressed over and over again . . . singing with perfect diction, purely and simply, without any fussy over-arrangements. I went to his dressing room afterward to tell him how much I admired his performance, and I commented on the handsome red velour robe he was wearing. Next day when I went in to rehearsal, there was the red robe, freshly dry-cleaned and hanging in my dressing room, with a hand-written note pinned to the collar. "Here you are, Lawrence. And best of luck always. Perry." What a nice, nice man.

Wednesday I was up by five in the morning eating breakfast, making some hard-boiled eggs to take with me so I could eat on the run if necessary, and scribbling notes to myself on my script, and long before the ten o'clock call I was back at Harrah's for rehearsal—but so was everybody else.

We did a full band rehearsal in the morning, with George alternately cajoling and shouting at the fellows. Watching him brandish his baton like a dueling sword, I grinned. George and I have very different styles of working. He yells, I talk quietly. He uses rather technical terms, I hum and sing to get my points across. In fact, the boys were so used to my type of leading that when George first came on the scene in the early fifties, I nearly had a full scale walkout on my hands. I hired George when we were still playing at the Aragon Ballroom on Lick Pier in Santa Monica, because I felt at the time that we needed a smoother, more professional touch. I knew from George's reputation that his solid musicianship and know-how were what we needed to underscore my ideas for arrangements. So I hired him . . . tall, slim, bursting with energy, a powerhouse personality.

And that was the trouble. The boys were used to my quieter style. If I didn't like what they were doing, I tried to tell them as reasonably and tactfully as possible. Not George! He exploded—and he wasn't above telling a certain musician that he just might find it helpful to go back to school and learn a little something about notes. All the boys were incensed, and at the end of rehearsal one of the fellows got so overwrought he followed George down the hall and caught up with him just outside the men's room. "Listen, you," he snarled, shoving him up against the wall, "we got along very well in this band for years before you came along and we can get along without you now!"

I called the boys together after that. "Gentlemen," I said, "let me say something. I know you're used to the way I talk to you and this new man is . . . well . . . rougher than I am. But he's a brilliant musician and I have a hunch his bark is a lot worse than his bite. He can help us a great deal, so I'm going to ask you to cooperate with him till we find out if we can't get along together. Would you be willing to go along with me on that?"

Well, of course they were, and within a matter of days everyone had discovered that George's anguished outbursts were just George, and that he screamed so much only because he cared so much. He gave us the lift and direction we needed. Today, if he didn't groan and clap a hand to his brow in total despair from time to time, we'd think something was wrong.

Now, as we began moving right down to the wire for our opening night, he was in a frenzy of last-minute polishing. He was up and down the stage steps a hundred times, listening from every corner of the house, changing, modifying. I was doing the same thing while Jim serenely pulled all the loose ends together as he directed the entire production. We broke for lunch and returned immediately for a full-scale dress rehearsal, and then Rose Weiss, our costume designer, took her turn running up and down the stage steps. She'd dash out to the front of the house to take a look, run back up to adjust a hem or tighten a belt, dash downstairs to urge the wardrobe girls to sew a little faster or iron a little harder.

As the clock ticked on, the tension began to rise. There was that extra gleam in the eyes, that catch in the voice, the nerves that made some of the kids jump their cues. We worked up to the last minute and finished the rehearsal to the sound of knives and forks being rattled onto the tables in the background, as the waiters began to set them for the dinner show. I would really have liked to go over one or two of the numbers again, but there just wasn't time, so I called all the kids together at stage front while Jim gave them their instructions. "Now remember," he finished, "no matter what happens—keep going! If the lights fail . . . and they may . . . or you fall flat, just keep on singing. Don't stop! Okay, all of you back here, in full makeup and costume, ready to go, by eight o'clock sharp!"

I went down to my dressing room and got into my Perry Como robe and began to study my announcement cards, small white file-sized cards on which I made notes to cue myself in my introductions of the various members. I've gotten so dependent on cue cards during my years in television that I really need those notes the first few nights of any new run—otherwise I'd forget who's coming up next! (It could also be that I'm not as young as I used to be, but I prefer to think it's the cue cards.) After a few nights my mind settles down and begins to function a little better, but this night I was so tense and so tired I was afraid I wouldn't be able to remember my own name. I was sitting opposite a floor-to-ceiling mirror at the time and when I glanced up and saw myself reflected there, it scared me. I was so exhausted I was gray. My hair stuck out in funny little clumps all over my head, my glasses had slid down to the edge of my nose, and even my legs, sticking out from underneath the red robe, looked white and tired. "Oh, well," I thought, "no one can see me now." I read the cards one more time and then lay down and willed myself to take a short nap. I stretched out on the sofa under a light blanket and turned out the light. It was absolutely quiet, except for the faint sound of a saxophone coming from a rehearsal room at the end of the hall. Dave Edwards, I decided . . . maybe Russ Klein. The plaintive notes curled in the air and hung there, soft and lovely, sounds reminiscent of a hundred, a thousand opening nights over the years. All those nights from tiny little towns in the Midwest to big towns like Chicago, San Francisco, New York. That same overwhelming sensation of . . . "this is it, you can't back out now, everybody is depending on you." I wondered about our closing number. It was still too fussy, much too much arrangement. George liked a little embroidery, a little fullness in the background, while I was insistent on keeping the melody line absolutely simple at all times. It had been a continuing discussion for twenty-five years now and both of us were passionately dedicated to our own point of view. But if George was stubborn, he also had the best interests of the orchestra at heart, fully as much as I, and I knew it.

I couldn't sleep and finally I got up and got dressed. I knew that Lon was flying in from Nashville for the opening, and I wondered if he'd arrive in time for the show. If so, I'd like to introduce him. Fern would be there, of course, along with some house guests and our son, Larry, and his wife Tanya's parents, too.

Outside I could hear the tempo beginning to pick up, and I unlocked my door and threw it open, so that anyone who needed to confer with me would know I was awake. There was an air of supercharged excitement in the hallway as the kids milled around nervously, checking each other's appearance, exchanging quick hugs and kisses, wishing each other luck.

I could feel my own adrenaline starting to rise and at precisely eight o'clock I picked up my baton and started walking up the wide, red-carpeted stairway to the stage above. Harrah's produces all their shows with an attention of timing worthy of the finest television or radio shows, and at *exactly* eight-fifteen the curtain rises, and you'd better be there, ready to go!

I kept my eye on the clock and when it got to eight-twelve I went out on stage and stood behind the prop doorway through which I was to make my entrance. Everybody else was already in position, the fellows in the band dressed immaculately, instruments polished, music lined up on their stands, sitting tensely, ready to go. No matter how many times you go through it, an opening night is always an overwhelming experience, an unknown quantity which can only be discovered by plunging right in and measuring it. Suddenly, an announcer cut into my thoughts. "And now Harrah's proudly presents . . . Lawrence Welk and his Musical Family!"

The lights came on, the curtains parted, the band burst into the opening strains, the boys and girls in

the wings began to sparkle and dance even before
they came out on stage, and—standing all alone behind
my doorway—I, too, began to dance, all by myself,
the music acting like a shot in the arm, a strong drink,
releasing all the tension and worry and pressure that
had been building up for weeks. When my cue came
I burst through the door, hardly able to contain myself,
and when the audience applauded, I felt like ap-
plauding back!

It seemed to me that for an opening show, everything went quite well, but even as one part of my mind
was intent on the entertaining, another was making
notes on the things I felt needed changing, and the
moment the big gold curtains pulled to a close I
wheeled in my tracks and headed downstairs to my
dressing room. Around me on the stairs the boys and
girls chattered alongside, almost whooping with relief
that the show was over, chattering excitedly about
what had gone right and wrong. Cissy and Bobby,
our dance team, had had such a fast change to make
that Cissy's gold-mesh snood had fallen loose, and
one of Bob's suspenders had snapped open, threat-
ening him with peril at any moment! They needed
a slightly longer musical bridge to give them time
to get dressed and we discussed it swiftly as we ran
downstairs. That was just one of the little things that
needed doing, but most of all the show needed tighten-
ing, and I knew we had our work cut out for us in
the next two hours.

My dressing room was jammed. Every seat was
taken and so was most of the floor space. All my
production staff was on hand, plus Bob McClure and
Doug Bushousen of Harrah's—and all of them were
armed with sharp pencils and strong opinions as to
just what was wrong with the show. Just as we began
to work, Sam came in the door with Lon. He had
arrived in time to see the show and I was anxious
to get his opinion.

"It's too long," I began, as everybody nodded assent. We all knew Harrah's wanted a show under an hour and a half, preferably one that ran an hour and twenty minutes. Ours had timed out to an hour and thirty, which meant we had to cut eighteen minutes. Some of that would be easy, because it was time taken up with the extra introductions and speeches customary on an opening night. But some of it was actual show-time and that's where we really had to get down to work. It's always very difficult for me to cut anybody's number entirely. I know how very hard they have worked to perfect it. So I prefer to tighten a show by cutting an extra chorus here, a few bars there, an overlong production number here. That kind of cutting tends to pull a show together anyway, and give it more pace and brilliance. So we went right through the whole show, number by number, disagreeing only on which ones should be cut—and how much. Jack Imel lightened the tension considerably at one point, by volunteering to cut his number completely.

"But the audience loved it, Jack!" I objected. He and Arthur Duncan and Bobby Burgess had done a tap dance, in which each one had attempted to outdance the other, a routine made famous by the Step Brothers. "I thought it went over very well."

Jack grimaced. "Yeah, but I'm getting too old for that kind of thing!"

We all laughed. "Well, if you feel you're such an old man," I suggested, "why don't we capitalize on that idea? You can pretend you're too old to keep up with the other two. You know, run out of breath . . . things like that."

Jack made another face. "I won't have to pretend," he said candidly. "I *can't* keep up with them!" Nevertheless, he could see the possibilities inherent in the idea and he promised to give it a try.

"All right, gentlemen," I said, "I think that's it

for now. Let's see how good we can make the second show." Myron set off at a run then, to give the changes to the boys, and Jim did the same thing for our singers and dancers. I knew neither of them relished the job. All performers have strong egos or they wouldn't be performers in the first place, and having to give up or shorten a number is sometimes very hard to take. Nevertheless, I felt certain the kids would put the good of the show above their individual preferences.

I was very tired, almost shaky, but as soon as I began getting dressed for the second show I felt that familiar surge of energy. Lon waited for me as I got dolled up. "What did you think of the show, Lon?" I asked.

For a moment he didn't answer. Then he said slowly, "Mr. Welk—you have a very fine production. But I'll have to see it a few more times before I can give you any specific ideas." I nodded. I knew his criticisms would be very helpful. I also knew that he wouldn't say one word till he was sure of what he had to say!

It seemed to me that the cuts and changes did help the second show move at a much faster, brighter pace, and the "Buck dance" brought down the house. After I introduced Jack as the "old man" of the group, he bounced out on stage, full of vim and vitality and began to dance up a storm. The audience identified with him right away, and gave him waves of applause every time his turn came around.

But as the turns came faster and faster, Jack began to wilt, and finally, in spite of the encouraging applause and shouts, he shook his head and went over and sat on the piano bench. The other two kept right on dancing, occasionally tossing him a condescending smile as if to say . . . "Too bad, old boy, guess you can't keep up with us," and goaded, Jack staggered back, determined to join in.

But the pace was too much for him, and the act ended with Arthur and Bobby leaping in the air, beaming and smiling, taking bow after bow, while poor Jack crawled off wearily into the wings on his hands and knees. The audience loved it, and I could tell from their reaction that we were all well on the way to discovering a new piece of business which could be as successful for us as the "Wig Bit" had been in other years. It needed refining and polishing, but basically it was a very funny piece, and all of us were pleased. Even Jack!

It was after one-thirty in the morning when we sang the last note of our last number, "The Battle Hymn of the Republic," and those big gold curtains pulled to a close for the last time. Suddenly, all the fatigue and tension and excitement of that long, long day hit me. I was just exhausted. When I came out of my dressing room after changing clothes for the fifth time that day, Lois gave me an evaluation based on twenty-seven years of experience. "You," she said, "look tired."

"Lois," I said, "you are so right. I *am* tired. But I'll be all right in the morning."

I took the elevator to the stage level, walked up the long sloping ramp to the stage door, went out and got into the Rolls. It was raining, rather to my surprise. We had had such huge crowds for both our shows that it never even occurred to me it might be raining. I switched on the windshield wipers and the car radio, listening to somebody else's music for a change, as I drove through the soft warm rain. At home, I went straight to the kitchen for my usual after-the-show snack, but I was so tired I settled for just a glass of milk and a cookie.

It was three o'clock. I had a golf game scheduled for eight-thirty in the morning. Well, five hours' sleep should be enough. I'd better take my notebook along though, so I could jot down notes as they occurred to me. I was still far from satisfied.

I let myself quietly into the bedroom, got undressed

and eased myself into bed. Maybe, I thought, Myron's opening number could be a little brighter—more music, less talk. Maybe—suddenly I yawned so widely, and so unexpectedly, I nearly sprained my jaw! I just couldn't think any more. I sighed deeply, turned over, pushed my head into the pillow and almost instantly, I was sound asleep.

4

The Wig Bit

THE NEXT THREE weeks were heaven. Every day I played golf in that clean air and brilliant sunshine. I had a standing tee-off time at eight-thirty in the morning and Clay Hart or Guy Hovis or Johnny Zell or Jim Roberts or some of the other fellows often played with me. Everybody took advantage of the wonderful sports activities available. Bobby Burgess and his wife, Kristie, Myron Floren's daughter, went water-skiing every day—they had driven their fire-engine red sports car up to the lake with their own boat tied on behind—and the others either went hiking or swimming or horseback riding or fishing. Even Fern got into the act. Every day she drove into town and developed her arm muscles playing the slot machines! We were all astounded the first time we discovered this. Fern playing the slot machines? It didn't seem possible! But she not only played, she worked out her own "system," and I had a fine time teasing her about it until she began coming home night after night with her pockets full of money. At that point I stopped teasing, and started counting.

Those three weeks in the sun not only replenished our physical energy, they restored some badly needed self-confidence. We had turnaway crowds every night, with long waiting lines in front of the theater. It was very heartening and made us feel that our forthcoming tour would be equally successful. There was only one cloud on the immediate horizon, and that was the same one that had bothered me earlier—our booking at Madison Square Garden. The ticket sales were still lagging.

Lon and I talked about it before he flew back to Nashville. He was using a six-weeks' advertising campaign for our appearance at the Garden, incorporating newspaper, television, and radio ads, and I knew that if anybody could pull it off for us, he could. But when some of the others in our organization got a look at the advance sale, they urged me to cancel the booking entirely. One of them pointed out that ours was basically a "home" show, a "family" show, and New York just wasn't that kind of town. "And if you bomb at the Garden," he added flatly, "you'll have a black mark you'll never be able to erase." His words made a lot of sense to me, and I expressed my concern to Lon.

He listened and then said simply, "Well, Mr. Welk, it's true, you do have a 'family' show. But there are families in New York, too . . . just like anywhere else. And I know that once people find out you're coming to the Garden—they'll be there!" His Scotch jaw suddenly jutted out and his eyes glinted fire. "And I'm going to make sure they *do* find out!" That was enough for me.

Meanwhile we continued to work on the show constantly, smoothing out the rough spots, trying out new things, and it began to pick up the brightness and rhythm that mean you've got a good show. Every production begins to develop its own rhythm, and if it flows along with the kind of highs and lows that alternate pitches of emotion with more relaxed intervals, then you know you've got a pretty good one. Ours did . . . with Ralna providing the high spot of the first half when she sang "How Great Thou Art." Almost every night she brought the audience to its feet with tumultuous applause. And in the second half, Jack and Bobby and Artie moved the audience to tears of laughter with their Buck dance. In fact, it threatened to rival the popularity of the "Wig Bit," which had previously been our all-time laugh-getter.

When I first began to write this book, I debated about telling the story of "The Wig," but since I had made up my mind to tell all about how we run our show, the good as well as the bad, the disappointments as well as the triumphs, I realized I had to confess the whole thing! You may know what I'm referring to, particularly if you attended one of our personal appearances during those years.

The "Wig Bit," as we've always referred to it, produced the biggest, longest, loudest laughs of any in my fifty years' experience. Russ Klein, who used to be with Red Skelton, and consequently knows a good laugh when he hears one, timed the laughs one night, and one of them ran one minute and twelve seconds—and that's a long, loud laugh.

Strangely enough, the whole thing started almost by accident. One night, at the Palladium Ballroom in Hollywood, I called two polka dancers on stage to demonstrate their distinctive style for the audience. There's nothing unusual about that. I often walk back and forth on stage during our weekly dances, looking for good dancers to feature, and these two were exceptionally good. The girl, whose name was Janice Kuric, was a pretty blonde, and the young man, dressed in cowboy boots and pants, was named Bob Gerlach.

After they came up on stage, I asked Janice if she wouldn't like to dance with Bobby. "Well," she said demurely, "I'd rather dance with you!"

"Oh, really?" I said, beaming. "Fine!" I handed my baton over to Bobby, and the band started to play. But while I was still counting . . . "ah-one and ah-two" . . . and getting ready to start, Janice was already dancing all by herself, bouncing up and down in my arms, while I just stood there. After a second or two of this, I shouted, "Hold it boys, hold it! Stop the music!" Janice stopped dancing and turned pink. "What's the matter?" she asked uncertainly.

"Young lady," I said, as severely as anybody can speak, while looking at a very pretty blonde . . . "let me just tell you one thing. In this band, *I* do the leading!"

Janice turned scarlet and hung her head while the audience roared, and once again I gave the orchestra the downbeat. But again Janice got carried away, and while she didn't actually start dancing, she did start bouncing up and down with such enthusiasm that I finally said . . . "Stop pumping! Wait for me!" Janice collapsed against my chest with embarrassment, and the third time around she waited till I was good and ready, and then we began to polka across the stage. She was an excellent dancer, brimful of high spirits and vitality and we did fine until she suddenly grabbed me around the middle and began squeezing me like an accordion! That was too much. Breathing hard, I led her over to Bobby. "You take her!" I said, shaking my head. "This girl's too wild for me!"

While Janice was catching her breath I invited the other dancer, Bob, to take a whirl with Cissy . . . and he nearly brought down the house! He danced like a cross between José Greco and a North Dakota bucking bronco, tossing his long black hair back out of his eyes, stamping his heels and whirling Cissy in such a mad dance she could hardly keep up with him. The crowd cheered and shouted its approval and when Janice and Bobby finished up by dancing together in one of Bobby's expert whirling polkas, the house erupted with applause. I was delighted. Time and again we have stumbled across unexpected talent in this way, and these two had given all of us a rare time. When they turned up again the following week, I was very pleased to see them.

At the time, we were preparing our new show for

our cross-country tour and one of the numbers had Bobby and Cissy doing their polka and inviting members of the audience to dance with them. It occurred to me that Janice and Bob might add a great deal to the number if they came up out of the audience as "volunteers." I asked them if they'd like to try it when we first appeared at Tahoe. Since Janice was a school-teacher, she was off in the summer, so it fitted into her schedule, and Bob was also free to go. I thought their appearance would add a little fillip to the program and I was so right. It added the biggest little fillip we've ever had—but it happened purely by accident.

That first night, Janice came up out of the audience along with other volunteers. (And by the way, we never have any trouble getting people up on stage to dance—it's the other way around really.) Janice and Bob stood quietly with the others until it was their turn to dance and once again Janice got big laughs with her eagerness to start dancing without me, and Bob brought the house down with his wild polka. But this night, after Janice and I had finished, and I had said weakly, turning her over to Bobby, "Take this girl, she's too wild for me!" something happened that none of us had anticipated. Bobby began whirling Janice in a wild series of spins, and the two of them went faster and faster and faster—when suddenly, the air was literally split with laughter! I don't think I've ever heard such a scream in my life. Poor Janice's wig had flown right off her head, sailed way out over the audience and landed smack in the middle of one of the tables. Scarlet, Janice grabbed for her head, which looked almost bald under the strong lights, looked frantically around the stage for some place to hide, and finally darted under the piano. Meanwhile, one of the waiters had retrieved her wig, which hung from his hands like a limp kitten, and he dashed up and gave it to Bobby, but no amount of coaxing, either from Bob or me, could lure Janice out from under that piano. Finally Cissy took the wig and, crawling underneath, she helped Janice get it back on. Janice slunk out to the biggest ovation of her lifetime. We stood together at the microphone at center stage . . . Janice with her head on my chest, me stroking her wig . . . (very carefully, I might add. I didn't want to knock it off again!) . . . and finally, the audience calmed down. Bobby and Cissy led her offstage and back to her table on the floor amid great applause, and from that moment on . . . the "Wig Bit" was an essential part of our show.

Janice was a good sport about it. I don't imagine there are too many young ladies who would willingly flip their wigs in front of thousands of people every night, but she did, and she did it with great finesse. She never overacted, which is the great temptation of the amateur. She was just shy enough and sweet enough and awkward enough to make her character completely believable, and she continued to tour with us for the next two years. Bob, likewise, got the same reaction, and he also, unintentionally, built a great laugh for us when I asked him if he was free to travel with us. "Would you be in a position to travel with us?" I asked him in front of the Palladium audience.

"Well," he hesitated, "I don't know. I kind of hate to leave right now."

"Oh," I said. "Why? What do you do for a living?"

"Oh, I don't do anything," he said confidently. "I'm on welfare."

He was, too, but he decided to come along with us anyway, and Bob and Janice provided us with one of our biggest high spots. But, of course, we were unable to use them more than once in any one locale, and that's why I am, at last, forced to reveal that the two "amateurs" you may have seen with us, were really performers. We used to hear the audience arguing about it later, and we received a great deal of mail on the subject. It was about evenly divided with half the viewers thinking they really were volunteers and the others convinced they were part of the show. Over the next two years we added to the "Wig Bit" a good deal. Janice, who ordinarily wears glasses, began to wear them on stage, and she always handed them to me and I tucked them into my breast pocket. At the end of the act she always "forgot" her glasses and had to come back for them. And one night I inadvertently referred to Bob Gerlach as Bob Garlic . . . and that, too, got such a laugh we kept it in. As with most things in my life, we learned by doing, and we polished our timing and lines so that by the time we had to take it out we had it down to a fine point. I would say that one of the biggest reactions we ever got . . . aside from that initial appearance in Tahoe . . . was in Cleveland, Ohio, where there are such marvelous polka dancers. They are so good I was afraid maybe Janice would get lost in the competition. But both she and Bob reduced that huge audience in the Cleveland auditorium to hysterical laughter, and Janice made her exit that night by clutching her wig and running down the long center aisle of the theater and right out into the street. Two nights later she performed it for the last time. I hated to see it go. It had given a lot of people a lot of laughs.

Toward the end of our Tahoe run Bill Harrah gave his annual sitdown dinner for us, in his own home. With husbands and wives, that added up to over a hundred people, but Bill's dining room handled all of us very easily. In fact, he once told me that he had built it especially for us, and every year, when I see that spacious room and those beautifully appointed tables, I am reminded of that all over again. And grateful.

I was really very encouraged by our Tahoe engagement. It seemed to me we had successfully managed our first big step on the road back to television. And if our personal appearance tour turned out to be equally successful, it would be of tremendous help to us as we started off our new television season. That, of course, was what we were really aiming for—a successful return on television. Everything else depended on it. Our Tahoe booking, our road shows, our recordings, our dance dates at the Palladium . . . everything depended on the television show. And we were all well aware of it.

We had three weeks off between Tahoe and the beginning of the tour. Most of the fellows used the time to go back home to Los Angeles and get their families settled. I used the time to go back home and worry some more. "Oh, Lawrence, will you cut that out," groaned Don. "Now, look—Sam and I will worry about the sponsors. Lon will worry about the tour. And Jim and George will worry about the television show, so that doesn't leave anything for you to worry about anyway!"

I grinned. "Okay, Don," I said. "You do the worrying." (Then, just in case he didn't, I kept right on!)

The night before we left, Shirley invited Fern and me over for a family dinner and it was ten o'clock at night before I got started packing. I always pack my suitcase myself. If I let Fern do it, it would be so neat I couldn't find anything. I have my own method. After everything else is in, I cram in a lot of extra books and pamphlets. The books are to read if I get a spare moment, the pamphlets—which have to do with the training and sharing system we use in our organization . . . are for any media people who might be interested. Then I throw in the real essentials—an extra pair of reading glasses, several large yellow legal-sized writing pads, a goodly supply of pencils—and some emergency packages of cookies. And I'm ready.

I was extremely anxious to get going. This would be our first tour since the cancellation, and my first real chance to thank some of the wonderful people across the nation who had given us such instant and unbelievable support. Music is, and always will be, my life. No question about it. But music that cannot be heard is not truly music, and it has been our wonderful fans who have made our life possible. I wanted with all my heart now to thank them. And I could hardly wait to get started.

5

On Tour

FROM LON VARNELL'S FILES:
                LAWRENCE WELK
        SUMMER CONCERT TOUR
        1971 OPENING PERFORMANCE,
                AMARILLO, TEXAS
            AMARILLO CIVIC CENTER—
            SHOW TIME: 8:00 P.M.

FRIDAY MORNING, VERY early, I kissed Fern goodbye and headed for Los Angeles International Airport. It was gray and drizzly, hardly an auspicious day to begin a nationwide tour, but as we neared the terminal the skies began to brighten. Ted Lennon had picked me up, and now he pulled to a stop at the loading zone, handed me my suitcase, shook hands, wished me luck, and drove off. I looked around for a familiar face. "Over here, boss!" cried a cheery voice. "Right here!" I turned, and there was big Barney Liddell, surrounded by luggage, waiting to tie a bright-red "Lawrence Welk Orchestra" tag onto my suitcase. Barney, who also plays bass trombone in the band, is in charge of all our personal luggage on tour, making sure it travels in one unit so there's a minimum of delay or confusion. Jack Imel does the same thing for our scenery and costumes, while drummer Johnny Klein is responsible for the life's blood of our group— the band instruments. Without those we wouldn't have a show of any kind. All of our instruments and equipment travel in specially designed steel cases which weigh over 55,000 pounds when packed, and I sometimes wonder how the plane can take off with a load like that.

"Everybody's here, boss," said Barney, twisting the tag onto my old green suitcase. "I think we're ready to go!" He beamed, brown eyes gleaming, smiling as always, even at that early hour in the morning.

Inside the terminal I found Lois waiting, along with Sid Bracy, the travel agent who sets up all our tours, and, of course, Myron. No matter where we go on tour, Myron is always at the airport ahead of everybody else, handing out our boarding passes, smiling, relaxed, easy-going, an oasis of calmness in a frantic world. I've never discovered how he gets there so early, but he manages it somehow, and his smiling face is always a reassuring sight.

We use every variety of transportation on our tours—airplanes, busses, or private cars—and we fly every variety of plane, too, from DC 9's to 747's, on chartered flights or regularly scheduled commercial lines. On this very special morning, however, we took off in a big and beautiful Continental 727. Most of the kids sat together in the center section, the girls wearing jeans and sweaters or blouses, the fellows in comfortable tee shirts and doubleknit slacks. Everybody does his own favorite "thing" to pass time on board. A good many of our kids read—I would say Mary Lou Metzger and Bob Davis are our two biggest readers—while others settle down for a nap. But most of them talk and Tanya is our champion talker. You can always hear little shrieks of laughter coming from her corner of the plane. I sat down and did what I usually do—work! Lois hauled out the morning collection of letters and I dictated replies as we took off. Afterward, I wandered around the plane. I love people, and one of the things I like about traveling is the chance to talk to so many varied personalities. I can learn a lot. Sometimes, though, if it's an especially long flight or I'm overtired, I find a couple of vacant seats, stretch out and take a quick snooze.

But not this morning! We were all too excited to sleep, thinking about the big tour that lay ahead. I studied the itinerary Lon had forwarded to me: Amarillo, Jackson, Atlanta, Knoxville . . . a long series of dates in the South . . . then a cut-back up into the North and Middle West, and then a general move east till we reached New York City. My heart skipped a beat when I saw that date sandwiched in between Pittsburgh and Boston where we'd be playing the big Boston Gardens. After that we would play a few more dates in Ohio and Indiana, winding up in Evansville before flying straight back to Los Angeles and our syndicated debut. It was an excellent schedule, worked out with the exact attention to detail for which Lon is famous. He had promised to be waiting for us at the Amarillo airport when we arrived, and I knew he would be there without fail.

I looked around the plane. Charlotte sat reading, trim as always, in a pants suit. Arthur Duncan was also engrossed in a newspaper while the girls were in a huddle giggling and talking, Sandi's bright red hair catching the morning sunlight. Across the aisle and down a little were Ralna and Guy. When Ralna first came into our office in Santa Monica to audition for me in 1969, I decided instantly that we had found a winner, and signed her immediately for the show. The funny thing is that Guy was along with her, too, and he also played the guitar and performed—but I didn't seem to hear a note he sang! I think Ralna's hazel eyes got in the way or something. And I do remember thinking that his hair looked awfully long. At any rate, after Ralna joined the show she kept telling us what a great singer Guy was. Finally I agreed to listen to a duet they had worked out and they came down to my backstage office at ABC and sang "Little Toy Train" for me. My jaw dropped when I heard them. They were wonderful! Guy had an unusual, plaintive kind of voice and their blend was perfect when they sang together. I got goosebumps just listening to them and immediately scheduled them for our Christmas show. The response from listeners was just as positive as mine had been, and Guy became a member of the "family" right away. They are our first husband-and-wife team and are, without question, the most popular performers we've ever had. Both are from the South; Guy's from Tupelo, Mississippi, and Ralna from Lubbock, Texas, and one day I mentioned that I'd hired more girl singers from Texas than anywhere else. "Well, sure, and I know *why* you hire them, too," said Guy, deadpan. "Because they're prettier, that's why!" I laughed, but I think he has a point. The girls in Texas are beautiful. In fact, I think Southern girls are unusually pretty anyway. They have a softness and charm you don't often find, perhaps because so many of them are "home" girls. But before the ladies in the rest of the nation get mad at me, let me say that there are beautiful girls in every part of the country! Girls in the North, for instance, have an independence and sparkle about them just as delightful as the Southern charm. I guess the truth is there are pretty girls everywhere—and that's fine with me!

I was glad we were opening the tour in Texas. Texans are famous for their friendliness and warmth, and if we played a good show in Amarillo it would get the tour off to a fine start. Watching Guy and Ralna as they talked quietly together, I wondered if they were remembering that it was just a year ago, almost to the day, that we had flown into Texas for another very memorable occasion—the celebration of Ralna English Day. That had been one of the most exciting shows we'd ever had, extra exciting for Ralna, of course, and we had all teased her beforehand, telling her to be sure not to cry. She'd tried not to, but the funny thing was that before the evening was over, we were all crying!

The excitement that time started to build from the moment we landed in Lubbock to find a large crowd on hand at the airport with a huge bouquet of roses for Ralna and a red carpet stretched from the plane steps to the terminal. Ralna had been almost overcome at the sight of so many of her friends, and when she found they even arranged a mini-parade into town, with a special perch on the back seat of the lead convertible just for her, she had a hard time holding back the tears.

Later, when she walked into the Lubbock Club for a luncheon which Lon and I had arranged along with her friends Monette and David Ince, and Naomi Caddell of the Lubbock *Avalanche-Journal*, and discovered that she was the guest of honor, she really did get tears in her eyes, because the whole thing was a complete surprise to her.

But it was the show that night that got to all of us. You could almost feel the surge of affection and regard coming from the audience. The auditorium was jammed, including two busloads of fans who had driven in from Spur, Texas, a small town about fifty miles away, and the place where Ralna had spent her growing-up years. That was enough to make her feel pretty sentimental, and when she walked on stage to prolonged applause from the audience, and found all the kids on stage singing a special version of "Hello, Ralna" to the tune of "Hello, Dolly," the tears began to sparkle in her eyes.

But Ralna is a complete professional and she managed not to cry even when the Mayor of the city, Dr. James Granberry, presented her with the key to the city and a Red Raider hat from Texas Tech. But when her own family joined her on stage at the close of the show it was too much, and I don't think any of us will ever forget the sight of Ralna standing close beside her father, holding tightly to his hand, and singing "Stand by Your Man"—while the tears just rolled down her face. Beside her, her father had a terrible time keeping his emotions under control, while out in the wings both Guy and I bawled unashamedly. "She usually sings that song to me," said Guy, blowing his nose mightily, "but I don't mind if it's her Daddy." He then proceeded to cap the whole evening by walking out on the stage, thanking the people of Texas for producing "a girl like mine," and singing "My Cup Runneth Over." That did it! By that time everybody was in tears—Ralna, her mother, her father, the audience, the kids in the cast, Lon, me, everybody. But they were tears of joy. The show in Lubbock had been a tremendous success. If we could do half as well at our opening in Amarillo in just a few more hours, it would be a wonderful way to start the tour. I hoped we could.

I dozed a little, sitting in my window seat, thinking that a tour is something like living in a tightly closed vacuum bottle. So many things are crammed into it, it threatens to explode at any moment. Times and events and feelings and schedules get so mixed up and jammed together that the tension is terrific, and it takes a great deal of stability to stand up under the pressure. I had every confidence our kids could do it, however. And in spite of the bone-crushing weariness that sets in after awhile on any tour, I knew none of us would give it up for anything! The thrill of performing to live audiences, the warm and friendly faces we see all across the country, the unbelievable concern for our welfare that is displayed at every stop, are just so wonderful we are all touched and warmed by it. And too, there's a certain kind of closeness you develop on tour that you just can't get any other way. By the time you've traveled from one end of the country to the other, wedged together in planes, busses, or cars, shared dressing rooms at state fairs that were originally built to house cattle, stood on outdoor stages shivering in the wind or rain, or sweltered in hundred-degree temperatures—believe me, you build up a rapport that works—or else! And so far, ours has always worked.

Next to me, singer Ken Delo suddenly interrupted my reverie, snapping shut the book he'd been reading and putting it into his flight bag. "Are we getting close, Lawrence?" he asked, peering out the window. "This country look familiar to you?"

"Yes, it does," I said. "Very familiar." These Texas plains not only looked familiar, they brought back some very pleasant memories. I had started my career as a young bandleader in this part of the country, during the oil boom days of the twenties, playing in towns like Odessa and Wink and Midland. Later, I had played at the Lubbock Hotel, and then gone on to Abilene, where I played lunch and dinner music for a man named Earl Guitar. And our son, Larry, was born while the boys and I were playing an engagement in Dallas in 1940, so every time we book a date in Texas it's like going home again.

I buckled my seat belt as the plane began its slow descent. Far off in the distance I could see the town begin to take shape. When I first played Amarillo in the early thirties, it was a small frontier-type town. Today it is the railroad and commercial center for the Texas Panhandle, but it still has that wonderful, breezy, Texas-style friendliness which was apparent the moment we landed. There was a big crowd of fans to meet us, with such wonderful smiles of welcome it made us feel good right away. And Lon was there, too, just as he'd promised, tall and trim, looking fit as always, his eyes startlingly blue in his sunburned face. "Welcome, Mr. Welk," he called, "welcome sir!" He guided us quickly to a planeside conference where I chatted with reporters and some of the nice folks who had gathered to meet us, and then he hustled me off to a waiting limousine while the kids climbed aboard an air-conditioned bus. Everything moved like clockwork. Traveling with Lon is almost pure pleasure, because he has everything under control. I don't have to worry about anything but doing my job. I never worry about flight times or hotel accommodations or cars or meals for the kids, or what's the best route to the auditorium. Lon does it all, and he does it with such flawless perfection he makes it look easy. But I know from long experience what a back-breaking job it is! I also know the reason everything comes off so smoothly is because Lon has already put in hours and hours of preparation long before we see him.

Jack and Barney and Johnny went immediately to the Civic Center to make sure the sound and lighting were adjusted for our needs, and the band risers and props were in place and ready. Lon had already checked out the arena months before, something he does in every theater, auditorium, or forum we play on tour. That's just one of the things he does to insure a smooth trip. His job was simplified in Amarillo, because the Civic Center there was a brand-new, beautifully equipped building, able to handle almost any type of show.

After lunch Lon and I went to an informal news conference with some of the television and business leaders of the city, and a great many of them wanted to know why I was trying so hard to stay on television when I didn't have to. I explained again, as I was to do many times in the next few days, that I not only felt a responsibility to the kids on the show, but to the fans who had done so much to support us. "As long as my health holds up," I told them firmly, "I'm going to give our return the best try I can."

The conversations were very stimulating and I thought I could detect a note of real friendliness and encouragement in the questioners' voices. I would have liked to talk a lot longer but I saw Lon glance meaningfully at his wristwatch, and I knew it was time to leave and take a pre-show nap. That's something Lon absolutely insists on, and I learned long ago I might as well argue with a Marine drill sergeant as with Lon, when it comes to that nap! He knows from long experience that I love to talk to people and find it difficult to get away. He also knows I do a much better performance if I get a little rest before the show, so he's unyielding on that point. Lon looks as gentle as a lamb, but he has a way of saying in his soft Southern accent: "Uh . . . Mr. Welk, sir, I do believe it's about time for a little rest . . . ?" and before I know it I'm back in bed with the covers tucked under my chin, dutifully taking a nap.

We knew before we left for the Civic Center that night that the house was completely sold out, and when we arrived we found the demand for tickets had been so great that the management had added extra chairs on the catwalk, something that doesn't happen very often. We were all very excited . . . by the size of the crowd, by the fact that this was our opening show, by the friendly waves of welcome as we drove up to the stage entrance, by the Civic Center itself, which is a very beautiful building.

I really hadn't thought that anything could touch the warmth of our Lubbock show the year before, but the opening that night in Amarillo was just wonderful! Even the Governor of Texas, Preston Smith, and his lovely wife were on hand to cheer us on, and the entire audience was so responsive, so kind. They sat quietly, enjoying the soft guitar solo of Neil Levang, and then shouted with laughter when Bobby and Cissy brought some volunteers up out of the audience to dance the polka. Some of those dancers were just wonderful too, especially one couple who said they were from Muleshoe, Texas. ("MULEshoe?" I asked unbelievingly. *"Is* there such a place?" There is.) But the thing that impressed me most that night was the wonderful reception the audience gave our instrumental numbers. Every time the fellows played, especially something in the big-band style, there were waves of applause. Not the polite "we like it" kind of applause either, but the insistent, "we like it and want more of it" kind. We played a few encores and I made a mental note to feature more of that type of music on the upcoming TV show. More than anything else, the Amarillo show gave us our first clear direction on which way to go in our television series.

We were all stimulated by the excitement of that performance and the fact that, in Texas anyway, our fans still wanted to see us. We had had full houses in Tahoe, of course, every night for the previous three weeks, but that was a special case. In Tahoe people were on vacation, in a holiday mood, ready to go see a show every night if possible. But on the road it's an entirely different thing. There, fans must make plans long in advance to see a show, and make arrangements to get to the theater, perhaps driving a long distance. That's particularly true in Texas, where folks think nothing of driving two or three hundred miles to see a show. Everyone in a road-show audience must exert a special effort to be there, and to think we had been able to pull an overflow house for our first tour-appearance was the most reassuring thing that could have happened to us. It meant that even though a major network had fired us, there were still people who would go out of their way to see us, and I knew from their comments, they were looking forward to seeing us again on TV. It was a very good feeling.

We wound up the show in a blaze of sentiment, with everyone in the vast auditorium singing "The Eyes of Texas Are Upon You," and then we rushed around backstage getting things packed and ready for the next show. I stood aside as Jack Imel raced into my dressing room, grabbed my stage clothes off the rack, and my fancy white dancing pumps off the floor and then raced out again to put them in the steel cases for the flight for the next town for the next show. Some of the other fellows had specific jobs to do too, which they did quickly and efficiently, and then all of us crowded out the stage door and down the steps to the bus waiting to take us back to the motel. There was a big yellow Texas moon overhead, and a fine softness in the air, and smiles and happy faces everywhere I looked, and it made me feel so good and I had a hard time "coming down" from all the excitement myself. But Lon, who always radiates a soothing calmness anyway, got out some milk and ice cream for us when we got back to the motel and then the two of us just sat talking quietly for a while, enjoying our snack and relaxing a little. "A good show, Lon," I said finally. "I thought it went quite well."

"Yes, sir, it did, one of the best. And there was something very special about that show tonight, Mr. Welk," said Lon, suddenly serious. "There was such a feeling of . . . of closeness, of real affection. I always feel like it's a privilege to be able to present a show like that. I just thank the Good Lord for allowing me to be a part of it."

"I know. I feel the same way." We sat in companionable silence, finishing our ice cream, letting the tension drain away. I considered having another dish, but resolutely decided against it. "Well, Lon," I said, standing up and yawning a little, "I guess we're on our way. What's on schedule for tomorrow?"

"Jackson, Mississippi, sir. We leave at nine-eighteen in the morning. And there's a right nice golf course close to the motel, Mr. Welk. You might have time for a quick game."

I laughed, "Lon, how do you know all these things? Where'd you learn to be so efficient?"

Lon grinned. "Oh, I'm still learning, Mr. Welk. Still learning."

I thought to myself that I was still learning, too. And I expected to learn a whole lot more in the days that lay ahead.

6

Tom Jones, Elvis Presley ... and Me

WE CONTINUED TO play throughout the South for the next few days, and our reception was wonderfully encouraging. Sometimes I think Southern audiences are the best of all, but just about the time I come to that conclusion we'll play a date in the Northeast somewhere, and I decide they're the friendliest. I would say that the crowds in the South are the most polite, those in the Northeast the most aggressive, and those in the Midwest the "homiest." They're the quickest to invite you home for a chicken dinner or a ham breakfast. Those in the West have some kind of unpretentious friendliness. But it seems to me that the overwhelming majority of Americans everywhere, any time, are good, decent, thoughtful, wonderful people. At least the ones we meet are.

We played Jackson, Mississippi, where we did a "Pre-show" show. It was actually in Tulsa one time that I first got the idea for doing a Pre-show. That happened because we were scheduled for a two-thirty matinee, but by showtime the hall was half empty, with latecomers rushing in to take their places beside those who had already waited an hour or so. It was nobody's fault, just one of those things. We were playing in the beautiful new Oral Roberts University Auditorium, a few miles out of Tulsa, and the road leading out to the school was under repair. Consequently all the cars were being jammed into a narrow one-way lane. The monumental traffic jam that resulted not only tied up traffic, it sent everybody's temperature sky high! Including mine. It always disturbs me when an audience has to wait, and finally I could stand it no longer. I went on stage and announced why we were being held up and told the audience we'd try to entertain them till everybody arrived. So for the next half hour I played the accordion—if you can call that entertainment—and then Myron came out and lifted the level of performance with his accordion, Joe Feeney sang, and Bobby Ralston played a few organ numbers. The crowd seemed to enjoy it so much that it is now a standard part of our repertoire. Any time the audience seems to be having trouble getting in on time, we put on a Pre-show.

We played two performances in Atlanta, that lovely city with its parks and trees and Georgian houses, and then Knoxville, Tennessee, where our show had sold out almost immediately after the announcement was put in the papers. Much the same thing happened in Birmingham, Alabama, one year, where we also put on two shows. The Mayor, George Seibels, came backstage to visit me before the evening performance in the Birmingham Civic Center, and we both did a double take as he walked in the door, because both of us were wearing bright red pants. And wherever we played throughout the South, Guy always brought the huge arenas to absolute silence whenever he sang "Dixie" . . . and sang it right from the heart. Southerners are proud of their country, their fine old cities. One time when we drove by some beautifully kept lawns in front of the white Colonial houses in Memphis, I mentioned to Lon how neatly trimmed they were. "Why Memphis won an award as the cleanest city in the nation for two years in a row," he told me proudly. Lon isn't a Southerner for nothing!

DETROIT

We swung up north, and the days and the towns began to blur together. That happens on every tour, and looking back it's often hard to tell them apart. But a few places always stand out with crystal clarity— and some of them I'll never forget! There were a couple of things that happened in Detroit and Cleveland, one time, for example, that I have no trouble at all remembering!

Detroit was a standout from start to finish. When we arrived, a little after noon on a Sunday, we drove directly to the Hotel Ponchetrain, one of the most beautiful I've ever seen. There was French rosewood furniture upholstered in puffy satin in every room of our suite, with matching satin drapes at the windows, and great bowls of dark red gladioli on the tables. The windows opened out onto a spectacular view of the city with a glimpse of Windsor, Ontario, Canada, just across the river. The whole thing was so magnificent I had trouble getting to sleep, but I obediently lay down for my twenty-minute snooze while Lon checked out last-minute details. At one-thirty we walked a block and a half to Cobo Hall, where our matinee show was scheduled to be held. Cobo is one of the newest theater-arenas in the country, and certainly one of the most beautiful, a circular white marble structure with graceful columns. It looked dazzling in the sunlight, and it looked even better when we got closer and saw the tremendous crowds of people waiting to get in. Lon nearly exploded with joy. His blue eyes twinkled like headlights. "Well, will you look at that!" he crowed. "Will you look at that! I do believe we're going to have a full house this afternoon, Mr. Welk!"

At the hall he hustled me upstairs to my dressing room, vanished and then returned momentarily with a lady whom he introduced as Mrs. Helen White. Both of them were smiling broadly as if they were sharing a secret, and they ushered me down the hall and into another dressing room, where . . . with the air of a magician . . . Lon unveiled a cake which

Mrs. White had baked. I was stunned into silence at the sight of it. It was possibly the most beautiful confection I've ever seen, a huge sheet cake measuring about two by three feet. The crowning touch was forty-five little dolls which outlined the edges of the cake, each figure about three inches high, representing a member of our cast. Mrs. White had colored the hair of each of the girl dolls to match that of our girls, and made their features as similar as possible too, and she had fashioned the whole thing out of spun sugar. It was breathtaking, a real labor of love, and I tried vainly to express my thanks, but she insisted on thanking me! I just marveled at the goodness of people. Here she had worked, literally for days, to make that cake for us and all she wanted was the knowledge that it brought us some pleasure. After she left I could only shake my head in wonder. "I should be down on my knees thanking God every day for all these good people," I said to Lon. "How can I ever give enough thanks?"

The show that afternoon was electric with excitement. Detroit is Ken Delo's home town, and all his family and friends had turned out with our other fans in record numbers, filling the giant hall clear up to the topmost seats in the gallery. When you have a great big room such as Cobo—it seats ten thousand—and it's packed to the rafters with a happy and enthusiastic audience such as this one, then the applause seems to come in waves, like the breakers crashing on the shore, with one wave stimulating another until it becomes one continuous exciting roar of approval. It's the most wonderful feeling in the world to entertain a crowd as responsive as that one was, and I'll never forget it—nor will I forget what happened afterward either! In fact, it made me feel just like Tom Jones or Elvis Presley, and never in my wildest dreams did I ever expect to feel like either of those two gentlemen. But as we emerged from the stage door late that afternoon, we ran right into a tightly packed crowd of fans, mostly ladies I have to admit, and they seemed to get very excited when they saw me. I assumed they wanted my autograph and I tried to write a few, but the crush was so great I couldn't get my arms up. The ladies were pushing and shoving from every direction, with those in the rear shouting and screaming at those in the front to move, but the trouble was that none of us could move anywhere! We were wedged in too tight. Lon had had the foresight to hire a limousine and alert some extra policemen and guards, but the car was parked fifteen feet away from the stage door, and no matter how many times we surged toward it, we surged right back again. Concerned, Lon finally battled his way around in front of me and then, with his head down and his elbows up like a linebacker, he began battering his way through the crowd, with me right behind him. My writer, Bernice, who was with us for that show, was petrified at the onslaught and had a terrible time keeping up with us. "But I'm with *them!*" she kept shrieking at a policeman who was trying to shove her aside. By the time the three of us made it to the car my hair was standing straight up, my tie was under my left ear, my coat torn off, and my shirt pulled out of my pants. Even my shoelaces were untied. Lon shoved us in, jumped in behind us and slammed the door shut and ordered the driver to move. The poor man tried, but the density of the crowd made it impossible, and then to add to the excitement, the women began pounding on the sides of the car, rocking it back and forth and imploring us to roll down the windows for just a moment. Some of them even burst into tears as they knocked on the panes, crying and shouting.

Bernice was very impressed at all this. "Does this happen every time you go on tour?" she wanted to know.

Well, as a matter of fact it doesn't, but I wasn't about to let her know. I figured I might as well increase my mystique while I could. "Oh, absolutely," I assured her. "The women just go crazy whenever they see me. Happens all the time, doesn't it, Lon?"

Lon, who is a truthful Methodist, turned first pink and then red as he tried to figure out some way to answer me and still stay in good standing with his church. And me. Truth prevailed. "Well," he said finally, "it happens . . . sometimes."

I sighed. "Lon," I said, "sometimes you are just too truthful!"

From Detroit we flew directly to Cleveland. Lon was concerned over whether or not we'd be able to fill the cavernous Municipal Auditorium that night. "Cleveland's a sports town," he mused. "They don't go much for musical or theatrical events here, I just don't know." We checked into the Hollenden House and embarked on a round of press conferences and TV shows, and then Lon dashed over to the auditorium to check on ticket sales while I took my nap. When he tapped on my door to awaken me I got up immediately, took a cold shower, and dressed in my fancy pale blue double-knit suit with the pink shirt and tie (sometimes I wonder if I've come *too* far from the farm). When I walked into the living room raring to go, I found Lon looking almost stricken. "Oh, Mr. Welk, I got you up a half hour too early! The show tonight doesn't start till eight-thirty, and I thought it started at eight. Oh, my!" he mourned, "you could have slept another half hour!" He was so upset I burst into laughter.

"Lon," I told him with absolute truthfulness, "I don't mind a bit. In fact, I'm glad to know you can make a mistake just like the rest of us."

The extra time allowed us to walk the three blocks to the auditorium. All along the way people would halt, nod pleasantly, and then wheel in their tracks, and yell . . . "Hey! Is that really you, Lawrence?" Then they'd come over to wring our hands and bid us welcome to Cleveland. I thoroughly enjoyed it and when Lon checked the box office as soon as we arrived and discovered that every seat had been sold, he relaxed and began to enjoy the evening, too.

I explored the backstage area for a while, acutely conscious that huge auditoriums, such as the Cleveland Municipal, are beginning to disappear from the face of our cities across the land. It makes me feel a little sad, a little nostalgic to see them go. They have presented such great entertainment to Americans for the past half century or so. The Cleveland house is fifty years old and features a stage so vast that its edges melt into shadows, and its ceiling soars into the air over sixty feet. When I walked into the manager's office I felt as if I had stepped back in time. The huge roll-top oak desk was cluttered with the mementoes of years of performing, and the walls were lined solidly with yellowing autographed photographs of entertainment greats . . . Galli-Curci, Maurice Chevalier, Houdini, Jack Dempsey, Louis Armstrong . . . echoes of a wonderful past. There was a flight of curving cement steps with a black iron railing, leading to the dressing-room area upstairs, but I had the "star" dressing room . . . the only one on a level with the stage. The girls commandeered it for the second half of the show when they had several fast changes to make, and the moment I heard their feet pounding toward my door, I'd jump out of my chair, sprint outside, and wait till they made their changes. Then I'd go back in and reclaim my room for a while.

Frankie Yankovitch, the Cleveland accordionist, very famous for his rendition of "Just Because," joined us, along with a twelve-year-old youngster named Anthony Rolando who had met us at the airport earlier in the day. I had been impressed as much

by Anthony's good manners as by his superior accordion playing, and I had invited him to come along,
too. They made a tremendous hit with the Cleveland
audience, which knows a good accordion player when
it hears one—Cleveland is the home of some of the best
polka dancers in the world. In fact, they were both
so good that when Myron came out, he played like
he'd never played before! He was taking no chances
with that kind of competition. And after the show
I did something I rarely do on tour—went to a party.
Lon was apprehensive and kept murmuring about
my needing my sleep, but I wanted to see Frankie's
restaurant, and he promised Lon faithfully that he'd
have me in and out in an hour and I promised to
leave on time, too. Frankie stuck to his promise, but
I fell down on mine. I had such a good time, I ended
up playing the electric organ and dancing till one
o'clock in the morning. When we got back to our
hotel, it was still a beehive of activity, however, because
a ladies' musical sorority was holding a national con-
vention at the time. We could hear them singing in
the ballroom, and when we walked into the elevator,
we found one of the delegates standing in the corner
all by herself, humming an operatic aria. She was
a pretty little thing, about sixteen years old, wearing
a blue lace formal, braces on her teeth and a camera
in her hands. When she looked up and saw me she
stopped, practically in mid-note, and her jaw dropped.
"Oh, *no!*" she shrieked, "not here, not right in this
elevator! Oh, wow, it's *him,* oh, I can't believe it!"
Saying which, she began snapping pictures feverishly
and then handed the camera to Lon so he could take
a photo of the two of us. When she got off at her
floor she was still emitting little squawks and squeaks
as she staggered off down the hallway. "Oh, *no,* it
was really him, oh I must be dreaming, oh, oh, *oh!*"

I looked over at Lon and smiled a bit smugly as
the elevator droned on up to our floor. "Well, Lon,"

I said, polishing my fingernails on the lapel of my jacket, "I guess you might as well face facts. You've got a matinee idol on your hands!"

Lon got very busy opening the elevator door and steering me down the hall. "Now, Mr. Welk," he said diplomatically, "you've had a very busy day. Why don't you just get yourself a good night's sleep?"

At five-thirty the next morning, matinee idol or not, I got up, met Lon for breakfast in the hotel coffee shop, and then drove to WJW, the CBS outlet in Cleveland, for an early morning interview. I rather enjoy interviews, even when I run into extremely sharp reporters like Lou Gordon, who questioned me closely about my personal life in Detroit one time. Sharp questions put me on my mettle and give me a chance to talk about the issues or values which are so important to me, like the training of our young people. I believe so strongly in helping them get started early in life, developing their sense of identity and self-reliance, as we try to do in our own training program, that I welcome every opportunity to talk about it. Even at seven o'clock in the morning!

Afterward Lon and I drove directly to the airport to find all the kids already there, waiting patiently, neatly dressed, rested, ready to go. I was proud of them. Their real character was coming through more and more as we worked under these pressure conditions which were sometimes very difficult or tiring. They never complained, and I loved their teamwork. Nobody had to ask any of them to do their share. They all helped. Each of the boys packed his musical instruments carefully in individual cases after each show, and then brought them to Johnny Klein to be packed in the big steel instrument case. And they hung their band jackets or other costume changes in the assigned wardrobe chests, too, ready for transportation. The girls did the same, hanging their costumes on racks in the order in which they'd be removed at the next show, putting their slippers into little drawstring muslin bags provided for that purpose, repacking the feather boas and rhinestones and other props they'd need again. And all the girls became experts at makeup.

At home, during the television season, we have top-flight makeup men to do this pleasant job for them. But on the road it's up to them, and somehow, with only one small travel case apiece they appear on stage flawlessly made up, every false eyelash in place, pancake on, hair perfectly curled. I'm still not sure how they do it—after all, I'm only a man—but those little girls get off the bus at the theater looking about sixteen years old, no makeup, hair pinned back by a ribbon, wearing jeans or a simple dress, and one hour later they've turned into glamorous singing stars. I'm always proud of our girls and the way they look, and I try to tell them so, but I frequently say the wrong thing. I'm never sure, for example, just who is wearing a wig. Not Cissy, I know, her hair is too short. But one time I complimented one of the girls on her beautiful hair . . . I won't say who . . . and she grinned. "Oh, do you like it?" she asked. "Here, take it!" Saying which, she yanked her wig off! After that I thought I'd play it safe and the next time I complimented one of the girls I said, "My, your hair is a pretty color! Is that a wig?"

"No, it is not!" she said with fire in her eyes. "That's my own hair!" You can't win.

The girls are very close on the road, like sisters, helping each other get dressed and made up. One time I popped a button off my suit coat at the last minute and ran over to the girls' dressing room to see if they could help me out. There were screams of "Wait a minute, wait a minute!" when I knocked on the door, but shortly Sandi opened it, smiling widely.

"It's okay now," she announced. "You can come in!" There on the floor was Cissy, still in her sweater and slacks, pressing her red chiffon dance dress so there wouldn't be any wrinkles. Gail was fastening a string of pearls around Mary Lou's neck, Ralna was holding a mirror so Tanya could get her false eyelashes in place, and Charlotte was buttoning the last button on Salli's Gibson Girl dress. All of them were chattering nonstop and when I explained what I wanted, they all pointed at Mary Lou. "That's you, Lou!"

Since that night Mary Lou has become our official seamstress on the road, which makes us very happy, although I'm not too sure how she feels about it! But I think she feels fine. I think one of the reasons our show is as close and warm and successful as it is is because all of us want to help. We really care. We care about the show. And we care about each other.

7

Cornflakes and Ice Cream

MORE AND MORE in the days that followed, I became aware of the unusual cooperation and goodwill that existed in our Musical Family. From little Mary Lou and her button-sewing, on down to Jack Imel, Johnny Klein, and Barney Liddell, and the way they always made sure our equipment was in the right place at the right time, to the way the entire cast stayed on stage during intermissions to sign autographs when they could have been backstage resting . . . all the kids behaved with such spirit, such dedication, my heart was filled to overflowing.

I had been aware, even before we went on tour, of the unusual friendship and concern we had for each other, the extraordinary rapport—and I thought I knew the reason, too. But it wasn't till Lon and I began talking about it one night that I came to know exactly *why* we worked together with such total cooperation. He pointed it out so quickly I was amazed! Lon is a delight to talk to anyway, and I might say one of the reasons I enjoy going on tour so much is the chance I get to discuss things with him. To my mind, he has one of the clearest views of life and business I've ever encountered. A conversation with Lon is just like going to school. All my life I've had a hunger for learning, of course. In the olden days, I learned so much from George T. Kelly, who took me right off the farm and helped me make something of myself with his little show, The Peerless Entertainers. Later, when I had my own band, I used to spend hours with Tom Archer, the ballroom owner who knew more about the dance-band and ballroom business than anyone else I ever knew. I loved my work so much I wanted to learn everything about it. Today, it's Lon. He knows more about personal appearance tours than anybody else in the nation—if not the world—and his own standards of morality and thinking are so high, they elevate those of everyone around him.

So I always looked forward to conversations with him. We usually talked at night, after the show was over and we were back in our rooms relaxing for a while—and we really lived it up with a bowl of ice cream or cornflakes. We had just as much fun with our cereal and milk as we would with a Scotch and soda. Well, more actually, because neither one of us enjoy drinking, and Lon, who is an ordained Methodist minister, is a strict teetotaler.

Sometimes, if I was very hungry, Lon would rustle up a light supper for me, and no matter where we were, big city or small, two o'clock in the morning or not, he always managed to find something light, nourishing—and broiled! He never failed. In fact, as I often told him, if there was any fault I had to find with him, it's that he was *too* good at his job . . . and to me. He had everything organized so I never had to worry about a thing.

There was a time, when Lon first started handling our tours, when all this wonderful care nearly backfired on me. I got so I just went wherever he told me, beaming happily as he steered me up one hallway and down another, or in and out of press conferences with just a quick word to tell me where we were and what was going on. But one night in Bismarck, North Dakota, I invited one of my best friends, Buster Hogue of Linnton, up for a visit after the show—but for the world I couldn't remember my room number. A little later, Buster asked me what time we'd be leaving in the morning . . . and I didn't know. Then he asked me where we'd be staying in the next town . . . and I didn't know that either! It bothered me because I've always had a good memory for such things. When I was booking my own band, I could tell you every detail of every booking for a full year ahead, and now I couldn't even remember what time the plane left in the morning. Even so, I didn't get upset until a few days later, when I couldn't remember the name of the town we were in! That did it. "Lon," I said firmly, "I better start doing things for myself again. If I don't, I'm afraid I'll forget my own name." I was kidding, but that little incident underscored something I believe in with all my heart. If you stop doing things for yourself—you eventually lose the power to do them. By the same token, if you do too much for somebody else you are really hurting them, because you are weakening their chance to build a self-reliant life of their own.

Lon himself is a perfect example of this. He was born into a wealthy family in Adamsville, West Tennessee, but during the Depression his father lost everything. Lon was just a youngster at the time, but he tried his best to help out by doing any odd jobs he could find. One day he approached the town banker, Mr. Robert Smith, and asked for a job. "Well, I'm sorry, son," said Mr. Smith, kindly. "There just isn't any work here for you to do."

"But, sir," said Lon after a moment. "I didn't mean it had to be a job here in the bank. I'd be willing to do anything, anything at all to earn a little money!"

"I see," said the banker. "Well, in that case I do have a cow out in the pasture at the edge of town and the land is so choked up with bitterweeds it's affecting the taste of the milk. Would you . . . want to pull up those weeds?"

"Yes, I would," said Lon, and then, exhibiting the resourcefulness and business acumen that still distinguish him today, he added, practically, "How much does it pay?"

"Ten cents," replied Mr. Smith, probably expecting his young friend to back out.

"I'll take it!" cried Lon, beaming. "I'll get started right away. And thank you, sir, thank you very much!" And he sped out the door and on his way to the pasture at the edge of town where he got busy pulling up every bitterweed he could find.

It was a hot day and there were a great many of those pesky weeds and it was a backbreaking job, but Lon stuck to it until he had every weed pulled. He was just finishing up when the banker came out to see how he was getting along. Mr. Smith took one look at the superlative job Lon had done, and without a word handed over the ten cents. And then he added, "Lon—you've done a really wonderful job. You're a fine young man. And if you ever need any money in the future to get started on a business of your own—you just come in the bank and ask for it. You won't need any collateral. Your word is your bond."

A few years later, Lon did that. He needed money to launch a business venture and the bank immediately lent him the necessary funds, starting him off on his tremendously successful career. That banker did Lon a great favor, and he gave him much more than a dime's pay for a day's work . . . he gave him the chance he needed to get started in life. He taught him that we often make our own opportunities and the first thing to learn about life is how to earn it for yourself.

I loved that little story and I just loved to hear Lon tell it, too, partly because I remember so clearly my childhood days on the farm when we children were each given ten cents as spending money for the year, and the way I used to spend hours trying to decide how to spend one penny at a time. Then too, I loved to hear the way Lon's Southern accent curled around the words. (For those of you who may meet him some day, do me a favor and ask him to tell you the story of "the ten cents." I'm sure you'll enjoy his accent just as much as I do.) Most of all, however, I appreciated hearing this little anecdote because I believe so much in the philosophy it expresses. Lon believes, as do I, that learning to do things on your own and taking responsibility for them is one of the key requisites for success in any field. "Well, I truly believe that's one of the reasons your people do so well," he told me one night, as we sat together comfortably, talking . . . he with his bowl of cornflakes and me with my dish of ice cream. "They know they can go just as far and just as high as they've a mind to. The opportunities are there—all they need to do is take advantage of them. And they do," he added thoughtfully after a moment. "I would say your group is the most highly motivated, the very nicest I've ever worked with."

"You really think so?" I asked, pleased and a little surprised.

"Yes, sir, I do. And that's not just my opinion, Mr. Welk. I hear that all the time from others in the business, too."

Since Lon used to be a college basketball coach before he began working in the promotional field, he's had a unique opportunity to work with all kinds of people, and I value his judgments highly. I was so pleased with his assessment of our group that I began telling him in detail about the training and sharing system we use in our organization.

I've felt for years it's the real reason for our success, and for the good feelings we have for each other. Of course I'm also aware that I've been lucky enough to find people who really *are* exceptional . . . dependable, honorable, always willing to work beyond requirements. In fact, there are those who say I have some kind of sixth sense about finding and hiring people, a mysterious ability to smell out talent and character that other people miss. If I have, it's just that I've extended my natural powers of observation, something we all have. I think most of us can sense another person's strength of character pretty quickly. You can usually tell if people are putting on an act for you, and if you can't, it will reveal itself in time anyway. Sooner or later your innate qualities come out. You just can't hide them . . . and if those qualities are good . . . or in a condition so they can be built up . . . you can make them even better.

And I've also discovered that you almost always get the kind of performance you *expect* from people. I'm not talking about singing a song, or playing an instrument either. I'm talking about performing any kind of job with honesty and spirit and happiness. If you expect people to do a perfectly wonderful job for you, both as a friend and an employee, chances are they will. I always expect the best from my people, I let them know I believe in them, and nine times out of ten, they just don't let me down. That's a much better way of achieving than dressing somebody down. I never do that—unless I lose my temper! I have to admit I do once in a while, and when I do, the sparks fly. But I try to keep that to a minimum and by and large I think I've succeeded. I might say . . . (I seem to be confessing everything in this book!) . . . that conquering my temper has been one of the biggest jobs of my lifetime. I'm somewhat of a perfectionist, and my natural instinct is to be very irritated whenever anybody falls far below their own level of perfection. But I've learned over the years that human nature is human nature, and it's never perfect. So if someone tries to do his very best, we can't ask for more. We operate on that theory.

But there's a great deal more to our system than that. I would say the most descriptive word, the one that encompasses our real idea . . . is "sharing." That's not a new idea, of course, but we have taken the basic concept of sharing profits, and added some touches of our own which make the idea unique, sharing not only our profits but ourselves as well.

I explained all this to Lon. I gave him facts and figures describing in detail how the plan worked. I told him how we shared our dreams and our past experiences, as well as our profits, and how this seemed to develop a mutual affection and concern. I added that nothing gave me more pleasure than finding and developing a talent in our singers and dancers, giving them their chance in the limelight. I told him how all of us constantly brought in fresh ideas and suggestions to help the show succeed. I did pretty well at explaining to him exactly *how* the plan worked, but I fell down miserably when I tried to explain the underlying reason WHY it worked so well.

"It's as if I'm a father with forty-five children," I began. "I try to help my 'kids' realize their dreams —and they try to make me proud of them."

Lon nodded.

"And it develops real trust between us," I went on, searching for exactly the right words to say what I meant. "It makes the kids feel as if they are somebody 'special' . . . that we really believe in them."

"I see."

"But that still doesn't say it!" I cried finally, frustrated by my inability to express myself. "I know this works to perfection because I can see for myself every day of my life! But I just don't have the words to tell you why it works so well."

Lon sat silently for a moment and then he said, "Mr. Welk . . . what all of us need . . . every single one of us . . . is love, recognition, and a goal. We all have to have love, or we cannot live a fulfilled life. And we want to be recognized, too, not for what somebody else's idea of us is, but for what we ourselves are—or can become. And we must have a goal to give focus and meaning to our lives. That's why your plan works. Because it meets these primary requirements."

We sat in silence. I was very moved by his simple, beautiful explanation. After a moment, I said, "Lon, would you please write that down for me? I . . . I just never want to forget this lesson."

Lon smiled. "I don't need to write that down for you, Mr. Welk," he said gently. "You've got it written in your heart."

8

Fair Dates

WE BEGAN A series of fair dates. I have mixed feelings about fairs. Sometimes I love them—and sometimes I don't. It all depends on the weather. If we're playing on an open-air stage under a broiling sun which threatens to cook us where we sit, or in weather so wild and windy it nearly blows us off the stage, then no, I don't like them. And the thing that really "bugs" all of us is when we have to play in weather so cold we can't get the instruments in tune. That's really upsetting and I don't know who looks the most agonized then, me or the boys, as they blow sour notes that set all our teeth on edge.

On the other hand there are things I love about fairs—the holiday mood of the crowds, the beaming sunburned faces, the excitement, the friendliness. And there are times when we are playing under a big full moon in soft and scented summer air when I feel I'm just about as close to heaven as I'm ever going to get.

We had two days like that one time in Milwaukee, at their state fair. Things got off to a great start at the airport where we were met by the Kids from Wisconsin, a fifty-piece orchestral group who were scheduled to share the bill with us. They were all teen-agers between the ages of fifteen and nineteen, and they looked so good in their bright red band jackets and white skirts or trousers, and played so well . . . their brass section in particular . . . that I was almost worried about having to follow them!

Their leader, Mark Azzolino, drove me to the fairgrounds for the first of the two evening performances, and just as we drove in the gate, we could hear the house band playing our theme song, "Bubbles in the Wine." They hadn't planned it that way. They had been playing theme songs of all the well-known big bands, so it was just a happy coincidence that they had been playing ours, but it seemed very appropriate. I had a trailer dressing room set up close to the stage for that show and it was very convenient for me, but a power surge earlier in the day had blown out all the connections so that neither the kitchen nor bathroom facilities were working. Mark kept me supplied with constant pitchers of ice water, but the other "facilities" were located a block and a half away across a broad green field, and I broke all records sprinting over there and back between shows! It's amazing how fast you can move if you have to!

Midway during the first show Jimmy Roberts came out to do his song. As usual there was a concerted rush of ladies, armed with cameras, toward the stage. I don't know what it is that Jimmy's got, but whatever it is the ladies love him and whenever he appears—out come the cameras! One lady managed to edge her way very quietly right down the center aisle and up to the apron of the stage where she began snapping pictures of Jim from every conceivable angle, and she had such a light of adoration in her eyes that I leaned over to her. "Would you like to get a good picture of Jimmy?" I whispered. She nodded eagerly, and before she quite knew what was happening she was up on stage in front of twenty thousand people. I waved Jimmy to a stop. "This lady would like to take your picture, Jimmy," I said. "I think she has a crush on you." Jimmy laughed while the lady turned as pink as her linen dress.

"Well, I do like him," she confessed.

"Where are you from?" I asked her.

"Menomonee Falls," she replied. After Muleshoe,

Texas, I should be prepared for these names I guess, but I could hardly get my tongue wrapped around that one. "Menomonee . . . *where?*" I asked. "You're sure there is a place like that?" Half the audience shouted out that there was, about sixty miles to the north.

"If you came all the way just to see Jimmy Roberts," I told her, "then I think you should have your picture taken with him."

I had her stand next to Jim while I stood back to snap the picture and Jimmy once more began to sing his song "I Want No Other Love But Yours." But the two of them stood stiff as pokers so I came over and pushed their heads together and had them hold hands. It still didn't look right, so I came back and pulled Jim's arm around her shoulders and pushed them closer together as he kept manfully trying to sing. "Don't be so stiff," I urged the lady. "Snuggle in a little bit!" By this time, the audience was getting in the spirit of the thing—and so was my lady from Menomonee Falls! She began grabbing Jimmy around the waist, snuggling in and batting her eyes at him, while the audience shouted encouragement and instructions, and I hopped around, sighting off angles. Poor Jim could hardly remember the words, let alone stay in key, but he struggled onward—and suddenly, just as he reached the last note, the lady planted a big kiss on his cheek—and I snapped the picture!

In the roar that followed, Jim bowed quickly and ran off stage. "Wait a minute," I called after him. "Come back here! Jimmy! Now how many years have you been with me?"

"Fifteen," said Jimmy, looking puzzled.

"Well, haven't I taught you better than that?" I asked, reproachfully. "Are you going to walk off and leave this lovely lady standing here in front of twenty thousand people after you've just sung a love song to her? When you have a date with a girl and sing to her—don't you take her home?"

Jimmy, who must have one of the nicest faces in the world, grinned sheepishly and the lady burst into laughter. Then he bowed to her, offered her his arm, and escorted her back to her seat while the audience accorded them a standing ovation.

Watching the happy, laughing crowds applaud, I suddenly remembered the very first time Jimmy had ever sung to a lady while I took their picture. That happened under circumstances as different from that warm and pleasant evening in Milwaukee as it's possible to be. Many years ago, when the Lennons were still with us (and still so young that their father, Bill Lennon, traveled right along with them), we had been scheduled to do a show at the Moody Auditorium in Dallas, Texas, but flying in from Little Rock we had run into a storm of such great proportions we were unable to land. The winds were so violent—over one hundred miles an hour as I recall—that when our pilot tried to put down at Dallas airport the winds grabbed the plane like a toy, turned it over on one side and hurled it back up into the air again. All of us on board were terrified, and almost automatically the whole plane began praying out loud—something I never expected to hear my boys doing!—while the little Lennons burst into tears. Dianne got out her Rosary and began to say her beads and Bill calmed the girls down by having them put their heads down on their pillows. We headed back to Little Rock where the storm was fairly well blown out, and landed there, rather shaken to say the least. The pilots held a conference with the weather tower and the airport authorities, and they returned to tell me they felt we could land safely in Dallas by flying in from another direction. I was in a quandary. The safety of my boys and girls was the only really important issue, no question about that. But the pilots assured me that the return trip was safe, and I was accutely aware that ten thousand people were already seated and waiting for us at the Moody Auditorium in Dallas. Finally, we decided to try again, and I telephoned Lon who was waiting for us at the Dallas airport.

Once again we were airborne, and as we flew through the black skies and heavy rain toward Dallas, a thousand thoughts went through my mind. I remembered the night my boys and I had floundered through a blizzard driving from Rock Springs, Wyoming, to Salt Lake City, under conditions so terrible we had all feared for our lives. I had made up my mind that night that I would never expose my kids to any such danger again, and I prayed sincerely that I was doing the right thing now for everyone concerned.

All during the time we were battling to get from Little Rock back to Dallas, the audience sat patiently awaiting our arrival, and Lon kept them informed of our progress. After I called from the airport, he drove out to the auditorium and told the packed house, "Mr. Welk is on his way. If you want to wait for him he'll put on a full show as soon as he gets here. But if any of you would like your money back, I will be more than happy to refund it." Only three people asked for their money back. The rest of the crowd sat and waited while a local piano player and a Spanish singer entertained them.

Meanwhile, we flew closer to Dallas and, when the pilot announced we'd try to land again, our prayers doubled in intensity. We all buckled our seat belts tighter, braced our feet and got ready for the worst as the plane began to descend. But the pilot did an expert job and, coming in from the opposite direction, he rode the winds gently down until he made a perfect landing. When the plane ground to a halt, we all sprang to our feet and pounded each other on the back, laughing and shaking hands, hugging each other, while the little Lennon sisters sobbed in relief. Lon was waiting with a lineup of taxicabs and private cars to transport us, and since Jim Roberts and I were the first off the plane, he grabbed us and hustled us right out to the auditorium. I was damp and dirty and tired and still wearing my wrinkled travel clothes when I walked out on stage, but nevertheless I got one of the greatest cheers I've ever gotten in my life. "Would you like to wait till we change our clothes and get into costume?" I asked, "or shall we just go ahead the way we are?"

"Just get going," came the yells from the audience . . . and we did!

But for the first fifteen minutes nobody but Jimmy and I were there to entertain. I got my accordion and played and played . . . I felt like I was back in Strasburg again . . . and Jimmy sang and sang. We kept stalling for time until the rest of the cast arrived, and it was then, noticing a pretty lady angling around trying to snap a picture of Jim, that I first had the idea of calling her on stage and taking her photo with Jimmy. The whole thing worked out so naturally and so well, that we have often used it since, whenever we spot a lady with that familiar light of love in her eyes. And it really saved the day . . . or rather night . . . for us in Dallas! The rest of the kids arrived in twos and threes all through the evening, and as each new arrival rushed on stage, he met with a storm of cheers and applause. One by one the fellows in the orchestra arrived and it was just as if my whole life were being relived right in front of my eyes—first there was just me and my accordion, then enough of the fellows arrived to form a little five-piece combo, then a sixteen-piece group, and finally the twenty-seven-piece band we have today! Everybody was tired and dirty and disheveled, but so glad to be alive that I really believe that was one of our best shows! Since we didn't get started with the full band till nine-thirty, it was well after midnight before we finished. When we came out, the rain had stopped and there was a soft breeze in the air and the kind of calm relaxation that follows any storm. It had been one of the most eventful evenings of our professional life, and I think it's safe to say that we all included extra prayers of thanks before we went to bed that night. I know I did!

When we played the state fair in Sedalia, I invited Myron and Bobby Burgess to come along with me—Lon couldn't be with us for that particular show—and the three of us flew in, very early in the morning, in a private plane dispatched by Governor Hearne of Missouri. It was a beautiful flight. We darted between towering piles of clouds, watching as the sun rose and turned the clouds first purple and then violet, and then a light pink. By the time we landed in Sedalia, the sun was up full and the day promised to be bright and beautiful. We drove immediately to the fairgrounds where the annual Feeder Hog Breakfast was being held in a newly built open-air pavilion, surrounded on three sides by tents and campers of the fair exhibitors. All the ladies wore long-skirted gingham gowns with ruffled bonnets to match and the men wore frontier clothes, and Governor and Mrs. Hearne sat at the head table along with other state and local dignitaries, including Senator Stuart Symington. They presided over one of the best breakfasts I've ever had in my life. For a minute there I thought I was back on the family farm again! We had home-cured bacon, eggs, grits, fresh home-made bread and rolls, jams and jellies . . . I ate like there was no tomorrow.

Afterward, they auctioned off some of those prize Missouri hams. The top ham went for fifteen hundred dollars to a local restaurateur who turned right around and donated it to Governor Hearne, who donated it to me. I donated it to nobody! I know how good those Missouri hams are and I decided to take it home with me. I clutched that ham close to my breast for the rest of that day, ignoring all comments about one ham winning another. Later on, the Governor made a very moving speech. He was then finishing up the second of his two consecutive terms as governor and he was therefore ineligible to run again. He commented on this fact and added that he felt a little sad at appearing at his "last" fair. There was a hushed pause for a moment and then I stood up. "Governor," I said wisely, "I know just how you feel. I got let out a little while ago too!"

After breakfast the Governor and I played a fast round of golf at the Green Tree Golf Club, and then returned to the Hospitality House on the fairgrounds where Mrs. Loyce Askew, the Fair hostess, fixed me up with some homemade cookies and cold milk. And after a brief twenty-minute nap, I was off to the showgrounds to meet the kids, who had flown in to Kansas City, and then taken a bus to Sedalia.

What a great night that was! The biggest moon I've ever seen, air as soft as a rose, and the biggest crowd in the history of the fairgrounds. Thirty thousand people were jampacked into the stands. They were even hanging from the lighting tower constructed next to the stage and crouched along the edges of the stage and sitting on folding chairs all around the back and sides, too. The crowd was in a happy, festive mood and when Mrs. Hearne, the governor's wife, came up on stage to sing "Till There Was You," they loved it. They were so generous and responsive with their applause that I felt as if a warm breeze of love were coming across the footlights to all of us. As always, when a show as exhilarating as this one comes to an end, I am caught between happiness and sadness. It's a strange feeling, hard to explain, like a brief passing shadow extinguishing a light. But we had another beginning, another show—and another bus to take in a few minutes, too, for the hour and a half trip back to Kansas City and our motel for the night.

I sprinted down the long cement ramp to my dressing room underneath the stage, and changed while the boom and roar of the closing fireworks display rattled the walls. Myron came in and told me that arrangements had been made to fly us in a private plane into Kansas City. "Barney would like to go along too," he added, "and so would Bobby Burgess and Mickey McMahon, if it's okay."

"Wonderful," I said gratefully. The prospect of a swift plane ride instead of a long bus trip seemed very good at the moment. It had been a long, long day, starting at sunrise, and I was tired. "Let me have my luggage out of the bus, would you, Myron?" I called as he left, and he nodded.

After a few minutes I made my way to the car in which we'd ride to the airport to find that Myron, efficient as always, had stashed my old green suitcase into the trunk. But no ham. "Where's my ham?" I asked him. The two of us went back into the bus and there, tucked neatly under my seat, was my prize ham. I dragged it out and held it close. "I don't want to lose this," I advised him firmly. "Don't let me forget it."

Driving along in the warm soft air to the airport, I relaxed completely and would have fallen asleep if Barney hadn't talked nonstop all the way. "Barney," said Mickey with interest when Barney finally paused for breath, "is it true that you have a tape cassette where your tonsils ought to be?" Barney was so outraged that he stopped talking for the next ten seconds while the rest of us chuckled. The truth is we enjoy his entertaining talk and miss it when he stops.

But when we pulled up at the airport, even Barney stopped talking, because the place was completely deserted! There were hundreds and hundreds of planes there, behind the locked chain-link fence—but no pilot. We drove around aimlessly for a while and finally parked by the small, unlighted terminal building and got out to wait. Ten minutes went by . . . fifteen . . . and finally our driver said quietly, walking toward an outdoor pay phone, "Well, why don't I just make a few calls and check up on things?"

Another half hour went by while he called everyone he could think of. "I just can't raise anybody, Mr. Welk," he said finally. "I don't know what's happened to our pilot, and the referral service has no information." We were getting concerned because Barney needed to make a one o'clock plane connection. By now, of course, the bus had long since left the fair-grounds and there were no other flights scheduled out of Sedalia for the rest of the night. So there we were in the middle of the airfield in the middle of Missouri in the middle of the night—with all those planes and no pilot! It was so quiet and deserted and somehow eerie, the planes silvery and ghost-like in the moonlight, that I felt like the hero of an old Humphrey Bogart movie, only I hadn't the slightest idea of how to get us out of this predicament. I was just on the point of asking our driver to take us on into Kansas City, when a car suddenly rounded off the highway and headed in toward the airfield. All of us heaved a sigh of relief when not one but two pilots got out of the car and walked toward us. But our relief turned to dismay when they turned out to be Governor Hearne's official pilots who had arrived ready to fly him and his wife back to the state capital. The Governor was due to meet them at the airport in forty-five minutes.

After a brief pause, I explained our predicament. "Do you suppose you could possibly fly us into Kansas City?" I asked.

"I'll call the Governor," said one of them, and he did so immediately.

All of us waited anxiously as he talked with Governor Hearne. "If it's all right with you, sir," said the pilot, "we could fly Mr. Welk and his party into Kansas City and be back in plenty of time to meet you and Mrs. Hearne. Yes, sir. Yes, Mr. Governor, I'll ask him." The pilot turned to me, grinning a little. "Mr. Welk," he called, "the Governor says it's okay if you'll give him three strokes on your next golf game."

"It's a deal," I said instantly. "And thank him very much."

Within minutes all five of us, plus our suitcases and my ham, were ensconced comfortably in the governor's beautiful plane, fully equipped with radar, and big enough to seat eight people. The flight was smooth as silk, cutting through the air without a ripple, and the drone of the motors and Barney's comforting chatter lulled me right off to sleep, and I woke with a start when we landed at the Kansas City airport precisely fifteen minutes later.

"Thank you so much," I said to the two pilots as we unloaded our luggage. "You just saved our lives. You can tell the governor I'm willing to give him *five* strokes!"

Clutching my ham to my breast, I climbed aboard an airport bus and snoozed a little as we drove to our motel. Once there, however, I snapped wide awake. Because there . . . parked in front of the place, with all the luggage removed, so that obviously it had been there for some time, was the bus the kids had taken in from the fairgrounds! Their hour-and-a-half bus trip had taken less time than our fifteen-minute plane flight. Progress, I decided, is in the eyes of the beholder, and sometimes a fast flight takes longer than a slow drive. Or something. I was too tired to philosophize. I was too tired even for my cornflakes and ice cream, and that's tired! But I wasn't too tired to forget about my ham. I put it right where I'd be sure to remember it when I left next morning, and I very carefully carted it with me for the rest of the trip and all the way back home, where Fern took one look at it and said, "Lawrence, that looks like a beautiful ham, but it's not on your diet! Did you forget about that?" No, I didn't forget about it. I was just hoping *she* would! So I didn't get a bit of my beautiful ham after all. Instead I took it down to the office to share with the kids and I know for a fact that Ted and Lois got a share of it, but how far it went after that I don't know. I just hope that whoever got a bite of it will realize that that ham was hand carried all the way from Sedalia, Missouri.

We continued to play our fair dates and the tour went exceptionally well, even better than we had hoped, with many of the dates ahead of us sold out. But not at the Garden. With less than ten days to go, we had still sold only about eight thousand tickets—and eight thousand seats would be lost in an auditorium that held twenty thousand. I was concerned, particularly when I received a second phone call from a man in our organization whose judgment I value very highly. "Lawrence," he said uneasily, "I just had another chat with Sam, and he told me about the ticket sales to date at the Garden. Now I know you've had a lot of advice pro and con regarding your appearance there, but I want to add my two cents worth, too. Have you stopped to consider that you're coming in on Labor Day? That's traditionally the worst day of the year for any kind of show in New York! Everybody's out of town, it's their last chance to get to the beach or the mountains." He paused. "I'll tell you, Lawrence, if I were you . . . I'd cancel the booking. Take the loss and get out. It'd be better than failing publicly."

I thanked him for calling, but I was upset and I talked to Lon again. "What do you think, Lon? Do you think we should cancel?"

Lon sat silently for a moment and then he said, "Mr. Welk, I . . . no. I do not. I know it's a gamble but. . . . I still think we should do it! As far as Labor Day goes, well, I'm aware of that of course, but I've always thought that was a plus for us, not a minus. I think your fans would rather drive down and see your show in a nice, air-conditioned arena than they would to drive to a crowded beach somewhere. I've been planning on that."

"But what about this low ticket sale?"

Lon hesitated. "Well, of course I would have liked to see a bigger sale by now, Mr. Welk, that's very true. But it's not too far off my projections, and I've always expected the biggest sale to take place during this next week anyway. That's the way I've geared my campaign."

He went on to explain it to me in detail, and even though I had heard much of it before, I listened, fascinated. Lon knows all there is to know about his business, he's the best there is. He's handled so many diverse personalities, from Engelbert Humperdink to Glen Campbell to the Harlem Globetrotters, that he's become an expert on audience appeal. In our own case, he knows the kind of fans we have and where they are and how to reach them. He schedules our concerts at convenient times, and in places that are easy to reach, with plenty of good parking space and not too many steps. He tries always to keep the comfort and pleasure of the audience firmly in mind, as do I, and that's one of the reasons we work so well together. Now, as he told me about his final plans, I was more impressed than ever. "You remember those tapes you made for me? The ones where you invite the folks to the Garden to see you?" I nodded. "Well, I've bought time on news broadcasts in the area, and they'll be running all next week. I've spotted them on the news shows," he added, "because your fans are the type who listen to the news, they like to keep up with things. And in addition to the TV advertising, I'm running announcements in the newspapers in all the smaller towns around New York, like Garden City and Englewood Cliffs, because that's where the families live . . . and they're the heart of your audience, the ones we want to reach. And I'm arranging for busses for the older folks who may not want to drive in to New York alone, to make it a little easier for them." He took a deep breath. "And in New York, I've set up some very fine interviews for you, with people like Earl Wilson and Kay Gardella, folks like that, and I expect that to bring in a lot of last-minute walk-in trade, too. I'm counting on that!" His face was pale, but his blue eyes were just as resolute as ever. "Mr. Welk . . . I've said from the very beginning that once folks find out you're coming to New York—they'll fill that Garden to the very top! And I still believe that, sir!"

"You feel that strong, Lon?"

"Yes, sir, I do. I . . . Mr. Welk, I've told you before how I feel it's a privilege to work with you, because I believe in what you're doing and the kind of entertainment you present. And I believe the folks in New York are just as hungry to see good, clean entertainment as the folks anywhere else! In fact, I'd stake my reputation on it. If we bring your show in—they will come and see it!"

"All right. If you feel that way, Lon, why then of course we'll do it. We'll do the best we can."

We shook hands on it. We had committed ourselves, and there was no backing out now.

9

Louisville

FOR MONTHS, LON had worried about our booking at the state fair in Louisville, Kentucky. "There's no indoor hall to use, in case it rains," he fretted. "And the weather is so unpredictable at that time of year, too." Then he grinned and added, "But I talked to Sam about it and he just said, 'Don't worry, Lon. Lawrence won't let it rain!'"

I gave Lon a look. "Well, Sam has a lot more faith in my powers than I have," I said dryly. If it rained it rained, and there wasn't a thing in the world I could do about it.

And as we neared the date set for the fair it seemed a rather needless worry anyway because the weather stayed unvarying—it stayed hot! The temperature went up and stayed up, and when we played Milwaukee the night before, it was still breathlessly warm. But as we flew into Louisville the following morning, the skies suddenly turned gray and dark, with clouds that looked suspiciously heavy with rain, and sure enough, just as we skidded to a stop at the air terminal, the first big drops spattered wetly against the windows. "Oh my," said Lon dolefully, "look at that."

"Now, don't worry," I said as we disembarked. "This looks to me like one of those light summer showers that'll be over in a minute. Nothing to it." Which only goes to show you what kind of weather expert I am!

I had been scheduled to address a luncheon meeting of the Kiwanis Club at noon, and Lon had arranged things so I'd have a short rest at the motel beforehand.

97

But as we left the airport, Wilson Hatcher of WDRB, the station which carries our show, suggested I do a quick interview for them. I looked at my watch. "Well, I think I can work it in," I said. (I never miss a trick if I can help it!)

He and I drove on to the station while Lon went out to the Holiday Inn to check us in, and we met later at Masterson's Restaurant in downtown Louisville for the lunch. And I thoroughly enjoyed it, too. I've said it before and I'll say it again—the reason Southern people are famed for their hospitality is because they really *are* hospitable and gracious. You can sense it the moment you arrive in town, and the luncheon served only to intensify my feelings. The folks sang "My Country 'Tis of Thee" better than I've ever heard it before, and saluted the flag with a fervor that sent a tingle down my backbone. In fact, everything went swimmingly, including, unfortunately—the weather! By noon the rain was really pouring down, looking as though it planned to stay around a long time. Poor Lon was aging right in front of my eyes. We were seated at the head table on a dais enclosed by floor-to-ceiling windows, so even if he'd wanted to, he could hardly have avoided the distressing sight outside. And as the lunch progressed the skies grew blacker and thunder rolled and winds howled as the rain continued to beat steadily against the window panes. Lon sank lower and lower in his seat, unable to eat a bite. I leaned over to him. "Now don't worry, Lon," I whispered urgently. "Everything will be all right."

"Oh, my," he said, sadly. "My, my, my. Well . . . ," he sighed deeply . . . "what will be will be." And he turned and continued to look mournfully out the window.

Nevertheless, I really enjoyed the luncheon because I was speaking on our training system, and the guests asked such intelligent questions that, for me anyway, the time flew by. Afterward I gave two interviews to the Louisville *Times* and *Courier Journal,* while Lon continued to pace hopelessly back and forth, and peer anxiously out the windows every three minutes. Apparently, this strategy worked for him, because little by little the rain began to let up! And as we drove back to our motel, we could even see one small patch of blue showing triumphantly through the scudding clouds overhead.

I was delighted. It was easy enough to joke at Lon's worries, but I knew he had a tremendous amount of time and money and dreams invested in each of our appearances, and a rained-out show was no joke for any of us. I was very glad to see the skies clearing, and Lon was overjoyed. He sped on out to the fairgrounds to check the equipment, something he does wherever we play, and I went back to the motel for my nap. I considered skipping it but finally decided to go ahead. In view of what happened during the rest of that eventful day, I'm certainly glad I took that nap. Otherwise, I might never have made it!

At five o'clock I got up much refreshed and got dressed up in a spiffy new hunting-pink sports coat, white pants and a white shirt embroidered in rosebuds. I wished later I hadn't worn that shirt, because there were two small roses on the collar, all evening people kept sidling up to me and whispering, "Lawrence, you've got a spot on your collar!" I had gotten dressed in all that finery because we were due to attend a cocktail party hosted by the television station. I really didn't want to go, though. Cocktail parties are one of the things I dislike most in this world. In the first place, I don't drink. In the second, you can't really talk to anyone because there's so much chatter it sounds like a band playing ten different numbers at the same time. And to top everything else off, I seem to have the kind of face that attracts the drunkest person at the party who always comes over, grabs me by the lapels, and tells me a long sad story. And usually tells it to me all over again as soon as he finishes. So I try very hard to escape those parties whenever I can, but Lon assured me this one would be especially nice, and it was. They had even arranged to have a glass of cold milk for me, and I was having such a good time I hated to leave. But promptly at six forty-five we said our good-byes and headed for the fairgrounds.

I had noticed that Lon was acting increasingly happy during the party, and I'd wondered about it because he's a strict teetotaler. The minute we walked outside, however, I knew why. The rain had stopped completely and there wasn't a cloud in the sky! Instead, there was a wide expanse of clear blue, and a lovely summery scent in the air, the kind that ties up in your mind with gardenias and lilacs and the clean fresh smell of air after a rain.

"Well, now," said Lon jubilantly, taking a deep breath and looking all around. "Isn't this nice? The rain has truly stopped, and it's a lovely night!"

He was even happier when we drove into the fairgrounds. He had been concerned that, even though the day-long rain had stopped, it might have kept the fans home anyway, but here they were, turned out in record numbers. I looked up at the grandstand and it seemed to be undulating slightly because everybody was waving newspapers or fans against the now-deepening heat and humidity of the evening. The grounds of the stadium were a sea of mud, of course, after the heavy rains, and we had to drive very carefully through the thick gumbo to the temporary wooden stage close to the grandstand. The management had laid down heavy plastic sheeting around all the entrances and exits to the stage, and that helped somewhat, but even so it made for very slippery walking. They had also draped a bright striped canvas awning from the back wall of the stage to the overhanging roof of the grandstand. I knew it was there to protect us from unexpected raindrops, but I worried for fear it might affect the quality of our sound. If I had known then what was in store for us, I wouldn't have given that awning a thought. It wouldn't have made the slightest difference anyway!

At seven-thirty the orchestra bus pulled up, and all the kids began to pile out. Cissy was at the head of the line, and she was the strangest shade of green I've ever seen. Now I've heard of people turning green from envy or jealousy or something, but this was the first time I'd ever actually seen it She looked like a wilted lettuce leaf. "Cissy, what's wrong?" I asked her in alarm.

She looked greener. "I don't know, Lawrence. I think . . . I have a touch of the flu. D'you think . . ."

"I think you better go right back to the motel and go to bed," I told her.

"No!" she said instantly, her face taking on a little color. "If I can walk, I'll dance! But . . . maybe . . . you could cut my long number with Bobby?"

"Of course, and we'll cut your polka number, too."

"No," said Cissy again, and her chin came out. "No. I'll do the polka."

The polka number at that time was one of the strongest numbers in the show, and drew tremendous laughs. Cissy was vital to its success and she knew it, and she wasn't going to let me or the show down if it killed her.

Nevertheless, I was about to order her to go home when she turned around and sailed off toward the dressing room. I started to hail Jack Imel to alert him of this minor crisis and ask Mary Lou to stand by, when Ralna suddenly staggered up. She wasn't green—she was red. And she was so hoarse she could hardly talk. "Lawrence," she croaked . . .

"Stop talking," I ordered automatically. "Have you got laryngitis?"

"I've got something. I think I can do my duet with Guy, but I don't think I'd better try my solo . . ."

"No, no, of course not. Don't hurt your voice."

She nodded and wandered off toward the dressing rooms, coughing weakly. I could feel my own stomach muscles begin to tighten as I wondered what else could possibly happen, and I took a good close look at the rest of the kids as they filed by, but everybody seemed in good shape. I caught Salli Flynn by the arm as she picked her way across the plastic mats. "Salli," I whispered urgently, "Ralna's not feeling well. Do you think you could sing her solo?"

"Sure," said Salli instantly. "It's not in my key but I know all the words and . . . well, I'll do the best I can." No wonder I love those kids.

By show time it was completely dark with just a few stars twinkling in the deep blue of the sky, and as the kids bounced on stage for the opening number the top bank of spotlights came on. At the conclusion of the song, "Everything's Coming Up Roses," each of the kids was supposed to pick up a bouquet of roses and run out into the audience to give them to the ladies. But this time they ran into trouble. The house lights failed to come up and they couldn't see a thing. The girls particularly, in their long, trailing pink chiffon dresses, had great difficulty trying to climb the wooden steps leading up into the grandstand, and when Tanya stumbled there was momentary panic backstage. Jack Imel got on the intercom immediately. "Put up the house lights!" he ordered tersely. "The kids can't see, get 'em on right away!"

"We're trying, we're trying!" came the answer, a little testily, from the lighting booth at the top of

Tanya and I holding a map showing the creation of the
Lawrence Welk Syndicated Network. Each one of those dots
represents a station. Today we have 254 outlets,
and 24 stations in Canada.

Bill Harrah and Fern are standing on the terrace of Bill's lakeside home, Tahoe, with me and his aunt, Isabelle Briggs.

Here's our whole "family" on the pier below Bill Harrah's home at Lake Tahoe, Nevada, just after the beautiful dinner party he hosts for us every year.

Our musical director, George Cates, who was with me for close to twenty-five years before I discovered he was a ham.

Jack Imel, Arthur Duncan, and Bobby Burgess doing their "buck" dance. As you can see, Jack's just about to give up.

This lovely little Scotch-Canadian lassie looked so young for her years. When I asked for her secret, she said, "Well, I just do what you tell me . . . take Geritol!"

Opposite. I never thought I'd have to make a living this way. (After I got a closer look at this picture, I could understand why some of our fans didn't like me dressed as a hippie. I didn't like myself!) That's Arthur Duncan and Bob Ralston in background.

This is typical of the arenas and forums in which we appear all over the country. This one is the L. S. U. Assembly Center in Baton Rouge, Louisiana, where we often appear.

Ralna, being surprised and delighted by the presentation of
a Texas Red Raider hat by Mayor James Granberry of Lubbock,
Texas, during the "Ralna English Day" festivities on-stage
at Lubbock Coliseum.
Lubbock Avalanche Journal Photo by Joe Don Buckner

Perennial favorite, "Ladies' Man" Jimmy Roberts,
at an outdoor performance in Soldier's Field, Chicago,
getting ready to serenade one of the ladies from the audience.

IN MADISON SQUARE GARDEN
TONIGHT - LAWRENCE WELK - 8 PM

Playing the Palace or Carnegie Hall was the dream of every performer in the old days. Today it's Madison Square Garden, the "Tabernacle of Entertainment."

Notice how everyone is beaming? That's because this was taken during the first show of our syndicated series . . . and we're all so glad to be working! (Left to right: Joe Feeney, Arthur Duncan, Ken Delo, Guy Hovis, Bobby Burgess, Jimmy Roberts, and Dick Dale; Sandi, Salli, Charlotte, Ralna, Cissy, Mary Lou, and Gail.)

You can tell I'm overcome at something I'm seeing at the
Polynesian Cultural Center in Hawaii.
The young lady at my left was our guide.

Opposite above. Arriving in Honolulu, Hawaii, for our
"special." That's Ralna being greeted by a pretty member of the
Aloha Week Court, with Guy Hovis behind her, followed by
Norma Zimmer and Dick Dale. Lieutenant-Governor
George Ariyoshi is standing in group at the right.

Opposite below. As you can see, this hula was just too much
for me! Fern enjoyed it, however, and so did Sam Lutz (in white
open-neck shirt), and Mason Mallory, of Western Airlines,
who is directly behind him.
Star Bulletin Photo by Ron Edmonds

Fern and I on balcony of our suite at the Sheraton Waikiki in Honolulu, on our forty-second wedding anniversary.

Opposite. Our wonderful young dance team, Cissy and Bobby, with Bobby's father-in-law, Myron Floren. Bobby's married to Myron's daughter Kristie. That's really what you call a "musical family."

Big Barney Liddell almost broke down in tears when we
surprised him on-camera with a tape recorder, in honor of his
twenty-fifth anniversary with the music makers.
He knocked me out when he confessed he had never missed
a paycheck in twenty-five years.

This is one of my favorite pictures. I have just introduced
Larry Hooper to our studio audience for his first appearance
after his long illness . . . and he is receiving a standing ovation
as a welcome back, with half the audience in tears.

Arthur Duncan leading some of the kids through a jogging routine. That's Gail Farrell, Jimmy Roberts, Bobby Burgess, Norma, and Mary Lou, working out.

The Hotsy Totsy Boys of the Seventies. That's Bob Lido selling a song, backed up by Charlie Parlato, Jack Imel, Russ Klein, Richard Maloof, and Bob Ralston, with Bob Havens contributing some Dixieland Jazz on his slide trombone.

Our pretty girls . . . Charlotte, Norma, Gail, Ralna, Sandi, Cissy, Mary Lou, and Anacani. It's nice to be surrounded with such lovely ladies, even when you're seventy-one!

I don't know whether Neil Levang, our fine guitarist, is congratulating Clay Hart on getting through his song . . . or vice versa. They are both wonderful artists.

Once a year, on our Christmas Show, our Production staff
lets me sing one phrase from Jingle Bells ". . . what fun it is
to ride and sing a sleighing song tonight." Unfortunately,
I forgot the words, and it broke everybody up,
especially Gail Farrell and Mary Lou Metzger.

Our lovely Tanya and son "Buns". . . Lawrence Welk the Third.

Jack Imel came to us fresh out of the Navy. He has since developed into one of our most valuable members, acting as assistant producer as well as a versatile performer. Here he's dancing with Mary Lou. That's Buddy Merrill and Guy Hovis in the background, with one corner of Jimmy Roberts' ear visible at left.

Opposite. Years ago I hopefully bought this miniature accordion for my son, but he never took to it, so I'm still playing it. (That's my St. Anthony wristwatch I'm wearing.)

The day we broke ground for our Lawrence Welk Plaza
in Santa Monica, I walked behind the plow saying
"Giddap Horse". . . which would have been all right, only
the horse was a mule. *Larry Lee Photography*

THE LAWRENCE WELK PLAZA

Fern and I riding around the track of the famous Rose Bowl
in Pasadena, with Virgil White, president of the
83rd Tournament of Roses Parade.

Opposite above. There are about seventy-five members of the
University of North Dakota band . . . but you'll notice
I managed to end up close to the girls.

Opposite below. Here I am with Bernice McGeehan, who
has been so helpful to me in writing both this book and my
autobiography, *Wunnerful, Wunnerful!* She's a real pro!

What a wunnerful feeling to reach seventy and still have
so much going for you. You can see Norma, Ralna, Cissy, and
Gail in the front row with Myron, Jimmy Roberts,
Bobby Burgess, Dick Dale, and Ken Delo in the second row.
(Richard Maloof and Johnny Klein in background.)

the grandstand. "But we're having a little trouble up here."

Well . . . that was the understatement of that whole long, unbelievable night. We learned later that the lighting men ordinarily used only two spotlights for this grandstand, but in honor of our show they had decided to use four. The only trouble was they had never tried them out before and when they plugged them all in at the same time, the whole thing blew out. They were trying frantically to plug into an auxiliary power supply and keep things patched up for us as we worked, and they did manage to keep a steadily diminishing, grayish light on stage for a while. But for some reason the lights in the grandstand went completely berserk and for the next half hour they popped on and off with no apparent rhyme or reason. A light would flicker on in the topmost reaches of the gallery, and then flicker off. Two lights would blaze on over the box-seats and suddenly black out. Whole sections of the house lights would go on and off with such maddening frequency the effect was dizzying, and then, to top the whole thing off, the spotlights on stage turned a funny orange color, fizzled, sputtered . . . and died completely. The audience groaned in unison at this and I decided to try a little comedy.

"What's the matter?" I asked, stepping to the microphone. "Don't you people pay your light bills around here?" Nobody laughed . . . because nobody heard me. The sound system had gone out, too! When I realized what had happened, I began shouting at the top of my voice, at which point the sound suddenly came back on so loudly the people in the front began holding their ears, while those in the rear began yelling, "We can't HEAR you!"

I really don't remember too much about the next forty-five minutes . . . although Lon told me later with tears in his eyes, that I put on the best show of my lifetime. The spotlights continued to flicker on and off—mostly off—while the sound system alternately blasted everybody out of their seats or went down so low they couldn't hear a thing. I told jokes, I chatted with the audience, I played the accordion, I sang, I danced, I did everything but light matches so they could see us—and somehow we staggered on, trying to give a performance.

And the kids never complained. Not once. I'll never forget that. They went on and did their numbers as best they could, sang as loudly as they could to accommodate the sound system, groped their way backstage, slipped and slid on the plastic sheeting, giggled their way downstairs to the underground dressing rooms . . . where, I assume, they made up by candlelight . . . and came back for more.

Lon meanwhile was near a state of collapse backstage. "Oh, my goodness," he moaned. "I think you're the only man in the world who would keep on going at a time like this, Mr. Welk. You're a genius!"

Well, that did a little to help keep me going, I must say, but mainly I was determined that the audience somehow, some way, should be entertained. If there was any way humanly possible to give those good people an entertaining show, we would do it. I called on every resource I had accumulated over the past fifty years. By the time you've played barn dances, and wedding parties, and vaudeville houses, and thousands upon thousands of radio and television shows, you build up a kind of basic technique, an instinct that seems to propel you through incidents of this kind. I don't recall what I said, but I do recall getting roars of laughter, so evidently I must have said the right things. But it kept getting darker, and the lights kept fluttering with such maddening irregularity that I was getting almost desperate, wondering what to do next, when suddenly, just as Sandi and Salli started to sing their duet, the stage spotlights came on! All four of them. Blazingly, incandescently, brilliantly, beautifully, *on!* And they stayed on! I don't think I've ever heard such a cheer in my life. Roar after roar of rebel yells, waves of applause, shouts of joy. Sandi and Salli, who are very pretty girls anyway, had never looked more beautiful as they stood there in that glow. After the applause finally subsided, I stepped to the mike and said, "Folks—I'm really hurt. Do you know what you just did? You just gave the electrician more applause than you gave me tonight!"

From then on . . . everything went right. Salli sang Ralna's song, standing in the warm glow of the now-steady spotlight, and she sang it flawlessly. And Cissy went through her strenuous polka routine with Bobby, including dances with various members of the audience, and she did it with such spirit and perfection no one would have dreamed she was ill. I caught her just as she made her exit. "Cissy, that was wonderful!" I whispered. "But are you sure you're okay?"

She flashed me a smile. "Sure, sure! In fact, I think I've danced that bug right out of my system!"

How I love those kids.

As the show drew to a close we played "Dixie," and pandemonium broke loose. I always love to play "Dixie" for Southern audiences. They just love it and I love it, too. I love to see people truly involved and enjoying themselves. Lon always rushes out on stage and waves his arms wildly, joining in with such fervor that even if you couldn't hear one syllable from him you'd know he was from the South. We all enjoyed it. And then Jimmy Roberts, who is from Kentucky, stepped to the middle of the stage, and with the spotlight shading down to a pale blue so that it banked him in shadows, he sang "My Old Kentucky Home." And there wasn't a sound. That huge crowd came to its feet and stood, reverently silent throughout the song. There was a feeling of warmth and unity, of love, I suppose. These were people who truly loved their country, loved their state, and they showed it as they stood quietly and listened to every word of their state song.

I loved the audience. They had been with us through every moment of that harrowing show. They understood how upset we were, how anxious we were to give them an evening of pleasure, something to remember. Well, I'm sure we did that all right!

But the thing I remember most of all about that evening is the fact that after the show, hundreds of those in the audience clambered and climbed and slipped over barriers and plastic sheets and boulders and mud to get to my trailer dressing room backstage, and they came, not for an autograph or to complain or to visit—they came to apologize for the fact that the equipment had inexplicably failed and made it difficult for us to do a show. Now, how can you help but love people like that? We were all close to tears before the evening was over, and by the time we were back in our hotel room, coming down after the show, both Lon and I were drained.

We sat in silence for a while, eating our usual bowls of cornflakes and milk, with a side dish of ice cream, when Lon broke the silence.

"Well, Mr. Welk," he said, with that little twinkle in his eyes, "I guess I didn't need to worry after all! Sam was right. He said you wouldn't let it rain!"

I shook my head slowly. I had nothing to do with it. The Good Lord was watching over us.

10

Countdown

As we neared the date set for the Garden, the ticket sales took a sudden sharp spurt upward, and everything began to look much better. True to Lon's predictions, the sales moved from a low of eight thousand seats, up to twelve, then fourteen, and now—three days before our concert—close to seventeen thousand. Lon rushed in with a sheaf of papers in his hands to tell me about it. "Now, that's not spectacular, Mr. Welk," he added, barely able to repress the smiles of delight quivering around the corners of his mouth, "but it's . . . it's truly respectable, sir! And I still have hopes for a full house."

"Lon," I said jubilantly, clapping him on the arm, "I think that's wonderful. Just tremendous."

I was extremely pleased by the news. The entire tour had been successful beyond our best hopes, and if we could make an effective Garden appearance, too, it would be of enormous publicity value to us as we went into syndication. So Lon's news was a great boost. It even helped relieve our fatigue, and by now we were all getting a little tired. Those five o'clock in the morning calls seemed to come around earlier and earlier, and some of the kids could barely take them. I am always irritatingly cheerful at that hour in the morning though, and I was still running around knocking on doors and making sure everybody was up. One day when we were leaving particularly early, I went out and stationed myself at the top of the bus steps, ready to carol "Good morning!" to everyone as they arrived. But the first one to show

up was one of my horn players, and he was clearly in
no mood for conversation. He was bent nearly double
from the weight of a suitcase in one hand and a plastic garment bag over the opposite shoulder, and he
was also swearing a blue streak as he approached.
"Why the blankety-blank I ever got into this stupid
blankety-blank business, I'll never know!" he was
saying wrathfully to himself, as he heaved his garment
bag into a more comfortable position. "Leaving in
the middle of the blankety-blank night like this! Stupid.
Blankety-blankety-blank!" Just then he looked up
and saw me standing there, and I thought for a minute
he was going to faint. "Oh, my God!" he cried, clapping a hand to his forehead as his bag tumbled to
the ground. "Not you!" Resisting the impulse to say
pontifically, "Yes, my son?" I began helping him with
his bags. "Oh listen, Lawrence," he babbled feverishly,
as he scooped up his luggage, "I . . . listen, please
forgive me, I don't know why I was swearing. I never
swear, you know that, but it's just so blankety-blank
early . . ." He stopped, looking stricken, and I burst
out laughing.

"I'm not the one to forgive you," I pointed out.
"Better go to confession to someone else." He nodded,
and never said another word, swear or otherwise,
for the rest of the trip.

We use busses more frequently in the eastern part
of the country, which is so heavily populated we can
play cities located just a couple of hundred miles
apart. I like bus trips. They give us a chance to see
the countryside and have a little fun, too. I often
take advantage of the situation to make a speech
to my captive audience, but more often I pass out
candy or cookies which our good fans have given
us and we have our own musical party, as we bounce
along over the roads, singing together.

Mary Lou Metzger and our bass player, Richard
Maloof, even fell in love on the bus, or so they tell

me. I noticed that they were always sitting together and seemed to have a lot to say to each other, so I wasn't too surprised when they came and told me they were going to be married. And I figured if they could get along that well on tour, especially on a bus, then they certainly should have a very happy marriage.

The night before we played the Garden, we went to Pittsburgh. That brought back a flood of memories. It was in Pittsburgh, at the William Penn Hotel, that we made our first really successful big-time debut on New Year's Eve in 1938. It's where we got the name of Champagne Music and found our first Champagne Lady, Lois Best. In many ways it was a real beginning for us, and here we were, almost forty years later, still together, still aiming for a new goal.

We played the Pittsburgh Civic Arena and the house was sold out. That was reassuring, because Pittsburgh is a big-city audience if any place is, and I was still a little concerned that the New York audience might be too sophisticated for us, as I had been warned over and over. And yet I felt, deep in my heart, that the folks in New York were probably just like folks everywhere else; like those in Pittsburgh or Seattle or Dallas . . . or St. Petersburg, Florida, for that matter. Well, the folks there may be a little different, because St. Petersburg is one of the favorite retirement spots in the nation, and a great many of our "mother and father" fans live there. And they are always so good to us! I've always felt if we can't make it in St. Petersburg we may as well give up. So far, however, they have accepted us so well we always have to schedule at least two shows. The last time we played there, I arrived at the Bayfront Center for the second show and found two little white-haired ladies waiting for me at the stage door. When they saw me they both burst into tears, and both began talking at once.

"Oh, Mr. Welk," cried one, grabbing me by the arm and pulling me around to face her, "we flew all the way down here from Allentown, Pennsylvania, and now, . . ."

"Now," interrupted the second one, yanking me around the other way . . . "now we can't get in! Oh, we never would have chartered that plane and flown all the way down here if we'd thought we couldn't get a ticket!"

"Oh, please," sobbed the first one, spinning me back again, "you've just got to do something, please help us." Saying which, they both stood there, sniffling forlornly.

"Wait a minute . . . now . . . just a minute, ladies," I said, amazed by this story, and dizzy from being spun around. "You mean to tell me you two ladies chartered an airplane and flew down here from Allentown?"

"Yes, we did, we did!" they chorused. "And now we can't get in! Oh, please . . . can't you do something?"

I looked at Lon. "Lon," I said hopefully, "we can't let these good ladies fly all the way down here and then not let them in. What can we do?"

Lon looked harassed. "Mr. Welk, there is just not another seat available, sir. Every extra seat in the theater has already been set up." Then he stopped, just as upset by all the tears and pleading looks as I was. "Well," he said finally, "there are those two chairs in your dressing room."

"Then, that's it!" I cried. "I won't need them, just take them out and find a place for these ladies somewhere."

Lon got the chairs out of my room and set them up at the foot of the stage at one side, where the two ladies sat beaming and smiling through the whole show, waving with delight every time I turned their way. They weren't any more tickled than I was, however. I don't think I'll ever get used to the great affection and closeness the people show for us. It means the world to me.

The audience in Pittsburgh gave us the same kind of warmth and affection, although I don't think any of them had chartered a plane just to fly in to see us! But their wonderful response did hearten us a great deal.

Nevertheless, I couldn't sleep very well. Tossing and turning in bed that night, I suddenly noticed the way the moonlight was slanting in through the windows, and it reminded me vividly of the way the moonlight used to slant in through the narrow windows of the sleeping room I had shared with my brothers on the farm. Many a night I had lain under my patchwork quilt, watching the light move slowly around the room, listening to the quiet breathing of my brothers, unable to sleep a wink, because I was dreaming such big dreams. Dreaming about playing my accordion, standing on stage in front of a huge, laughing, happy, audience, appearing in famous theaters throughout the land. Tomorrow night I would be playing in the most famous theatrical arena of them all . . . the world-famous Madison Square Garden . . . fulfilling a dream I had held in my heart for years. And I honestly didn't know what to expect.

11

The Garden

D-DAY AT MADISON Square Garden started very early in the morning. We landed at Kennedy Airport, where my good friend John Malone, director of the FBI in New York, met us at the airport, and he and Lon and I drove into New York over the Van Wyck Expressway. It was already very hot, with only a slight breeze, but the sky was clear and very blue, and it seemed like an auspicious omen.

We were all excited as we drove into town, past the wooden clapboard houses in Queens, then the more industrialized sections of Jamaica, then the old buildings left over from the World's Fair of 1939 and 1964, and finally down into the Queens Midtown tunnel which runs underneath the East River. By the time we had emerged from the white-tiled tunnel on the New York side, the streets were jammed with traffic and the tempo of the city was beginning to reach full roar.

We drove directly to the Statler-Hilton Hotel. We had decided to stay there for two reasons: one, it was close to the Garden, and two, the manager was an old friend of mine, D. W. Carlton, whom I had known since my days in Texas, where I used to play for room and tips at the Hilton Hotel chain there. "Tex" and I had been friends for years and I was anxious to say hello to him, but first I wanted to see the Garden. "Just a minute," I said to Lon as we got out of the car. "I want to take a look at this famous place."

I turned around, and there it was. Madison Square

Garden, massive, enormous, a huge building made of black glass squares, gleaming in the early morning sun. This was not the Garden of the old days. This was the new Garden, sleek and modern, with one building in the front connected to another in the rear by means of an overhead arcade and leading to a third, round, peach-colored structure at the far end. I thought at first that this circular arena was the Garden, but it was the smaller Felt Forum which seats about four thousand people. The Garden itself is contained within the larger unit of the building, which also houses the Pennsylvania Railroad Station, and the entire complex takes up a whole city block, a towering, shining palace of glass—and a place where a goodly percentage of our fortunes would be determined in the next twenty hours.

"Okay," I said to Lon after a long, hard look, "let's go."

"Tex" had installed us in the kind of luxurious rooms I never will get used to, large living room, dining room, two bedrooms, closets galore, everything done in pale French blue with gold wash trim, beautiful rooms, but we paid them hardly any attention. We had too much on our minds. Lon had set up a series of important press conferences for me, and I talked into one microphone after another, and shook dozens of hands. From time to time I could hear Lon conferring on the phone with Al Grant, manager of the Garden—(and impresario of the box-office!)—and every time he did so, it seemed to me that his cheeks were a little pinker, and his eyes a little bluer. He said nothing, however, and I didn't press him. He and I had watched the ticket sales rise steadily over the past few weeks, from a low of eight thousand up to seventeen and one-half thousand. Our dream—a full house—would be twenty thousand. But that, I told myself, was too much to hope for. Lon had done a magnificent job and we had come to New York with a comfortably full house, and that in itself, in the face of all the dire predictions that we couldn't attract anybody, was something of a miracle. Nevertheless, I couldn't restrain a wild surge of hope that maybe our impossible dream could come true after all.

After lunch, John Malone drove me to a couple of interviews—one of them was with Earl Wilson—and then he rushed me right back to the hotel, on firm orders from Lon that I was to be given plenty of time for an afternoon nap. But I couldn't do it. We had worked so hard and so long for this night that I just wasn't able to relax. And I was unusually nervous, too. I wasn't even sure why. I have played literally hundreds of thousands of concerts in my time and, particularly during the last few years—I just don't get nervous. Excited yes, full of anticipation, "up" in every way. But not nervous in the sense that I was—well, scared, to put it very plainly. But right now, I realized, both to my surprise and a little amusement, that's how I felt. As scared as the night I made my debut with George T. Kelly in The Peerless Entertainers in 1925, and that night I had been so frightened that George told me years later he had been afraid I would faint. "You were green," he told me with a certain amount of relish. "Positively green!"

I decided to take a walk before my nap, and stepped out into the Thirty-third Street afternoon traffic which was an unbelievable confusion of cars and people and cabs and busses, the sound of the trains thundering into Pennsylvania Station across the street providing a bass note to the whole arrangement. The wide cement railing bordering the narrow strip of grass around the Garden was covered with people resting in the afternoon sun, men in shirtsleeves, women holding babies, oldsters dozing, several drunks stretched out snoring loudly, with no one paying them the slightest attention. I walked quickly around to the stage entrance, and after a startled look at me, the guard waved me in with an understanding smile. I guess he's used to seeing nervous performers come in and take a look at the arena where their fate is going to be decided.

It was quiet, as it always is in a theater which is completely ready for an evening performance. Jack and Barney and Johnny Klein had obviously already been there. The band risers were in place, all the costume cases had been set up, my clothes laid out in the order in which I would wear them.

I wandered on through the wide backstage galleries, noting the huge flats stacked up in one corner, the wild Calypso costumes hanging from movable pipe racks in another, ready for the show to follow ours. I could hear the muted shouts of stagehands in another corner of the building as they struggled to drag some heavy lighting equipment into place.

I walked into the Garden proper and stood in the middle of the arena. It was huge. Huge and silent, an oval-shaped room with rising layers of seats that curved out at the sides and back in again at the top so that the whole thing resembled the inside of a giant eggshell. The ceiling was covered with a circular grid of light tracks radiating out from a center section, with each track holding hundreds of spotlights capable of producing the most intricate lighting effects. There was also a ring of light booths at the very top with eight more powerful spotlights.

The stage was set up at the end of the room, a simple square, with steps leading up to it at each side, a velvet backdrop at the rear. Comfortable folding chairs filled the center section of the floor with two additional side sections. Everything seemed organized and ready. As always, the empty theater held that sense of excitement to come, of life being held in abeyance until the audience came in. I'm sentimental and I admit it, and all kinds of thoughts went through my mind at that moment. I have played in my share of big theaters and concert halls and clubs over the years, and some of them have been very grand indeed. But the Garden, even though it is functional and utilitarian, almost plain, has a grandeur all its own. I thought again of what Lon had once said . . . "It's a Tabernacle of Entertainment." And standing there in that empty, quiet, powerful room, I thought how very apt that description was. I felt the same sense of dedication and commitment and humbleness you sometimes feel in church, and I hoped with all my heart that we would do well that night. In fact, if truth be told, I prayed we would.

Then I walked back to the hotel and stretched out on the bed and went sound asleep.

Promptly at five Lon awakened me and I showered and got dressed in the clothes Rose had set aside for me to wear weeks before, a gray and black patterned jacket with a light blue shirt and tie to match. "Those colors will stand out on stage," she had told me. I picked out a hankie, stuck it in my breast pocket, and went out to meet Lon. He also was done up in his very best. Full house or not, Lon and I were dressed for an occasion!

Walking over to the Garden with John and Margaret Malone at seven o'clock that night, I had a strong feeling of joy, almost a current of happiness just shooting through me. All of us were wearing little plastic buttons which would admit us to the Garden. "Why do *I* need a button?" I had asked Al Grant at dinner earlier that night. "I'm IN the show!"

He laughed. "Listen," he said, "I need a button, too, and I run the place!" And all along that short walk we ran into friendly faces. People would light up when they saw us, as if they suddenly spotted an old friend, and they held out their hands to shake ours, just like folks everywhere, and I realized down deep inside that, New York or not, these were family folks, too, just as Lon had said—and there seemed to be an awful lot of them! It had taken me just a few minutes to make that walk in the afternoon. It took us closer to twenty minutes that night. But it gave me the lift I needed and some of my nervousness began to abate a little.

Backstage, Lon guided our little party to my dressing room where there were some press people and other visitors, and we chatted for a while, but Lon kept shifting from one foot to another and after a few moments he excused himself and dashed out the door. Five minutes later he dashed back in again, and his eyes were so suspiciously bright I knew something was up. "Well?" I said. His voice cracked with excitement.

"Mr. Welk," he croaked, grinning. "I . . . uh . . . well, there's a *very* long line of people at the box office! It's . . . it's a mighty long line!" He beamed so hard I thought his smile would fly right off his face.

"Really, Lon?"

"Yes, sir, Mr. Welk. Really!" He beamed some more and then said . . . "Uh . . . I wonder—would you excuse me again for a moment?"

"Fine," I said "John here will protect me!" We all laughed as Lon took off, and chatted about nothing and everything for a few minutes, but I was so nervous I couldn't concentrate. I wanted to know what was going on, so I opened my dressing room door and peeked out. Just as I did, the door of the girls' dressing room at the far end of the hall opened too, and the girls began walking down the hall toward me, on their way toward the stage entrance—Cissy, Tanya, Ralna, Sandi, Salli, Mary Lou, Gail, Charlotte—all of them pretty as princesses, wearing pale pink and lace chiffon gowns, so clean, so sweet, so lovely. My daughters, the girls in the family, girls I loved like my own. Each one in turn squeezed my hand and wished me well as she walked by, and then they floated on down the hall, excited, happy, laughing, so sweet. Bob Ralston walked by next, serious, flexing his hands. I could hear Joe Feeney vocalizing in another dressing room, and then Bob Burgess bounded out, smiling as always, such a beautiful performer, such a nice man. Suddenly, Lon burst into view at the end of the hall, running like a deer. He was almost incandescent with excitement. "Mr. Welk," he gasped, "come with me!" He was so excited and his accent was so thick I could hardly understand him. "Mr. Welk . . . ah . . . ah . . . ah have something to show you ah think you're going to like! Come on, follow me!" Lon used to be a basketball player and he's still in top form, and I flatter myself that I'm in pretty good shape, too, but I really had to hustle to keep up with him as he dashed down a wide hallway, pulled me into an elevator, rode up a few floors, dashed out into another gallery, around a bend and then out into a sort of inner lobby contained in the heart of the building. There he stopped short and said—almost reverently: "Mr. Welk—looka there!"

I looked. On the white glass marquee it said, in two-foot-high letters—LAWRENCE WELK AND HIS MUSICAL FAMILY IN PERSON, TONIGHT, and in front of it, blocking out part of the sign, was the wonderful, the unbelievable notation—COMPLETELY SOLD OUT!

We had done it. We had filled the Garden. We had filled an arena that held an audience of twenty thousand people, reputed to be the most sophisticated, most difficult, toughest audience in the world.

I stood there with the clatter and roar of the station and the noises of New York all around me and I looked at that marquee and I thought how wonderful it was. And I was just as happy for Lon as I was for us. He had worked so hard and so long to pull this off, and he'd done it in the face of a great deal of opposition from highly knowledgable men. "Lon," I said huskily, "that's wonderful. This is one of the happiest nights of my life."

"Well, now," he said, clearing his throat, suddenly all business, "you better hurry. It's just a couple of minutes to show time." We raced back to the dressing room where John and Margaret shook hands and wished me well and then went out to take their seats in front. All the kids were already in place. Lon and I walked out to the huge curtains hanging to the left of the stage, billowing slightly in the breeze, and slipped through them to stand in the darkened space at the foot of the steps leading up to the platform. Lon usually takes a position there wherever we play, so he can watch the show and check on the reaction of the crowd. I looked at my watch. Eight o'clock. Time to go on. I put my hand to my stomach, took a deep breath, and began to walk up the steps.

Nobody announced me. I had planned just to walk up the steps and across to the mike in the center of the stage and say . . . "Good evening, folks. I'm Lawrence Welk." But I didn't get a chance. As I reached the top of those steps there was a roar unlike anything I have ever heard before or since. From every side it pressed in on me, from the topmost rows of the gallery, from the floor beneath me, from the balconies behind me, a huge concerted roar of welcome that grew and grew and grew until it was like being held in the palm of a loving and friendly hand. I stood there in that spotlight and I knew I couldn't possibly say one word even if I wanted to. And as the roar subsided, a wave of applause took its place, and continued until I was almost helpless with emotion. Never in my life have I experienced anything quite like it. Nothing can ever quite top it. I felt pinpointed, focused, receiving a kind of warmth that was like a breath of life. I have always known that I am most truly alive when I am performing for audiences, communicating with them, trying to exchange with them what is in my heart. My work is my life, my joy, my reason for living, the thing that makes everything else worthwhile. And as I stood there in that spotlight, the focus of such wonderful love, such an exchange of friendship, I thought . . . "I'm home, I'm where I ought to be. Maybe in some small way we're doing God's work. And I hope we do it well."

We just couldn't do anything wrong that night! The audience responded with roars of delight and applause for everything. Even when my tongue got tied up worse than it had in years, they laughed indulgently. I tried to announce that the boys would play Woody Herman's "Woodchoppers Ball," but just couldn't get it out right. I have no idea what I finally did say—I never got it straight—but it didn't seem to matter because we were all weak from laughing by then. Cissy and Bobby brought the house down with their dancing. Sandi and Salli were a bigger hit than they were in Louisville. Joe Feeney stopped the show cold and brought everybody to their feet screaming "More, more!" Ken Delo and Clay Hart got screams of applause, and little Mary Lou and Gail Farrell, in their first big New York show, were a delight. At the intermission, Ralna, as usual, brought the huge arena to reverent silence with her solo, and then the house lights came on and I prepared to sign autographs.

But when I started to walk down into that audience I almost got scared, because it was the biggest, most enormous crowd pushing and shoving to get close to us that I have ever seen. Lon instantly sprang down onto the steps beside me as thousands and thousands of people began converging on the stage from every side, shouting, screaming, laughing at the confusion, shrieking happily over the din and uproar, some of them shrugging in amusement when they got jostled away from the stage, others determinedly shoving their way back in. I felt as if I was being smothered under the onslaught. I started to slip on the steps and go under but Lon and one of the security guards grabbed me by the arms and dragged me up the steps to the comparative safety of the stage, while the other guards, reinforced by some extra policemen, linked arms across the bottom of the platform to keep the crowds back and under control. The screaming and pleading never stopped. I stood on stage, my coat sleeves nearly ripped out, my hair disheveled, my tie under one ear—and I loved it. Jampacked or not, pushing and screaming or not, these were our friends and I loved them. I moved back to the front of the platform and began signing like a madman. Everywhere I looked I saw arms . . . a forest of them, all stretched toward me with a slip of paper at the end so that they resembled trees in full bloom. I began to get a little dizzy as I signed and smiled, and signed and smiled, but even through that maze of confusion, one curious, and very pleasant fact, began to emerge. There were a lot of ladies in the crowd as always, but there also seemed to be an unusually large percentage of young girls, girls in their late teens and early twenties, and a goodly scattering of young men. Lon had noticed this in other cities but it was far more obvious here. I loved it. The mothers and fathers of these youngsters had been our close fans and friends for a long, long time. It was nice to think that maybe some of their children liked me, too. I felt like a fond uncle.

After intermission we went into the second half of the show and, if anything, it was better than the first. Cissy and Bobby did their solo, and then we did the polka routine that had been such a hit with our other audiences from coast to coast. And the New Yorkers loved it. Afterward I stepped down into the audience for my usual dance with the ladies. I was a little concerned after that onslaught at intermission, and true enough, I was mobbed again. I remember in particular one lady who plowed in from the back of the group, just mowing aside all the opposition, cutting through the waves. The crowd parted just like the Red Sea and she came up and grabbed me and we did a fast polka. But then the ranks closed and the ladies began tagging in again. I think I danced with more ladies that night, in a shorter space of time, than I ever have before or since.

At the end of the show all the kids came back on stage for our finale. I'd never seen the girls looking prettier. The excitement made their eyes sparkle more than usual, their color was very high, and their red ruffled chiffon dresses stood out blazingly against the dark blue velvet backdrop as the whole orchestra and chorus stood together to sing our closing hymn, the "Battle Hymn of the Republic." I stood at the mike and said . . . "Folks . . . why don't you join in with us? Then you can always say that you used to sing with the Lawrence Welk orchestra!" There was an appreciative ripple of laughter as I gave the boys the downbeat. The kids began and they sang so well . . . so well! And as we began the second chorus I could hear one after another in that huge audience begin to pick up the melody and sing along with us. By the time we finished, the whole house was singing, twenty thousand people singing with real emotion, singing together in that moving, prayerful song. As with the roar of welcome that had greeted us, the sound of those massed voices, singing in unison, was something I shall never, ever forget. It made a fitting climax to one of the most exciting nights of my life.

Afterward I came back out on stage and signed autographs for a while longer. I wanted to do something, somehow, to let the audience know how much I appreciated their support, how very much they've meant in our lives. I went down on the steps with Lon beside me and began to sign again. At first everything was quite orderly, but as the crowd discovered that there was another chance to get more autographs, there was a sudden rush back toward the stage that really scared Lon. He pulled me back up on stage and as he did so, six of the Garden security men formed a cordon across the stage again to control the crowd. Again the forest of arms reached up, imploring, thanking, calling, shouting, laughing. And again I signed till my arm was ready to drop off. It was almost two hours later when Lon finally convinced me to leave. "Mr. Welk," he said, "I think you've done enough signing now. I'm getting tired!"

I laughed. "Lon," I said, "I could keep on for hours. This has been a great night. A great night!"

And it was. As Lon and I and John and Margaret Malone walked back through the Garden proper, through the deserted hallways and galleries and out into the warm, busy, early New York morning, I felt about as happy as it's possible to be. All the store fronts seemed to have an unusual glitter and glow, the cars honking had a friendly sound, even the people shouting angrily at each other in the traffic seemed pleasant to me. I was in such a happy glow that I nearly floated through the lobby and up to our rooms, and Lon and I plodded happily down the long carpeted hallway to our impressive State Suite at the end, with the two-o'clock-in-the-morning hush hanging heavily in the air.

Lon went in and got out the cornflakes and ice cream he had set aside in the small refrigerator earlier. The two of us sat down in the splendor of the beautiful living room and ate a dish of vanilla ice cream apiece, occasionally grinning at each other. "A great night," I said from time to time. "A great night, Lon."

"Yes, sir, Mr. Welk," said Lon. "A great night. This is one I'll always remember. More ice cream?"

"No. No, thanks . . . I'm eating too much."

"Lon?"

"Yes, Mr. Welk?"

"When can we play the Garden again?"

The next morning I was still floating on air. I went out for a walk, and . . . what a beautiful day! The sky was bright and blue, the sun shining brightly, the ocean breezes fresh and clean. I felt so good I wanted to sing, shout, run around the block, do something! Halfway down the street, I spotted a shoeshine stand, and just as I passed it, the man in the chair got up to leave. It's so hard to get a shoeshine anymore, that I went over immediately and took his place. He yawned and stretched as he stepped down to pay his bill. "Think I'll get myself a beer," he announced.

"Good idea," said the shoeshine man instantly. "Bring me one, too, will ya?"

A beer at nine o'clock in the morning was not exactly my idea of the best way to start the day . . . although a few of the farmers in Strasburg used to do it . . . but I didn't need a beer, champagne or anything else to lift my spirits! I was feeling much too good! So I just relaxed and let the shoeshine man, who neither knew nor cared who I was, rub the polish onto my shoes and snap his polishing cloth back and forth across the tips in a soft-shoe rhythm. Presently a man walked by, stopped, peered closely at me and then came over to thrust a piece of paper in my direction. "Sign this," he ordered. I signed, smiled, and returned the paper. Three minutes later another man came by and did exactly the same thing (except that he added a "please" to his request). The shoeshine man watched both these encounters in mystified silence, but after the second man left, he couldn't stand it. "Now why'd those guys ask you to sign your name?" he demanded. "What'd you do that for?"

"Oh," I said blankly, shrugging my shoulders a little. "I—I dunno." He regarded me suspiciously for a moment, and then went back to his polishing cloth.

"Well, there sure are a lot of screwy people out this morning!" he announced loudly, clearly including me in the group. "A bunch of real nuts!"

But not even shoeshine men who didn't recognize me, nor grumpy fans who did, could spoil my morning. I was too happy. And so was Lon, whom I had left delightedly figuring out the exact facts and figures connected with the Garden show. We had filled the house—that was twenty thousand, one hundred twenty-nine seats. There had been a turnaway crowd of perhaps a thousand. The early reviews had been excellent, and the comments of the crowd as they left the Garden highly complimentary. On every level the night had been a great success, and I felt that the press coverage would help us a great deal. There was one picture, taken while I was on stage that night signing autographs, with hundreds of fans holding up programs toward me, that appeared over and over again in newspapers across the country in subsequent weeks. And in almost every case the caption underneath the picture expressed surprise that we had been able to please such a cosmopolitan New York crowd. I have always thought that those pictures helped widen our TV audience, by attracting some listeners who would never have tuned in otherwise.

From the New York Garden we went straight to the Boston Gardens, and that was another wonderful experience. After the performance one of the security guards came to me and, with tears in his eyes, said, "I just want to shake your hand, Mr. Welk, and tell you what a pleasure it is to have your people here. You know, we get all kinds of shows here, and some of those entertainers—well, you wouldn't believe how they act. They call us pigs . . . thugs . . . it makes it so difficult to do a decent job. But your people

. . ." he shook his head in admiration . . . "well, they are just the nicest, most considerate we've ever had." Needless to say, I felt very proud.

After Boston we went to Fort Wayne, Indiana, where, with Lon's expert help, we broke the house records, and then wound up our tour with a flourish in Evansville. Then—a little wrung out, but happy in the way you are when you know you've done the best job you can—we flew home, ready to tape our syndicated show. I clasped Lon's hand as we prepared to part company at the crowded airport in Evansville.

"Lon," I said, "it's been wonderful, every bit of it. I just can't thank you enough!"

Lon nodded, his blue eyes very dark, his face a little pale. "Mr. Welk," he told me, "it's been the finest experience of my entire career. The very finest. I don't rightly know how to express myself, but I sometimes feel that the Good Lord arranged for us to work together. There are just so many good people in this world . . . and I . . . I do believe that most of them are your fans!" I laughed, but I kind of agreed with him. There *are* a lot of good people in the world, and a great many of them do seem to be our fans, and I was more than grateful that the tour had given us an opportunity to thank them personally for their wonderful support. And I felt now, that the best way of all to say "thank you" would be to give them the finest television show of which we were capable. I think we all felt that way.

PART THREE

12

Syndication

FAR FROM BEING exhausted when I arrived home, I was filled with fresh energy, the kind of creative excitement that just wipes out fatigue, and I felt absolutely confident that we would succeed in our new venture. Never once did I entertain the thought that we might fail. Not long ago someone asked me if I weren't nervous about those first few syndicated shows. I knew, of course, how crucially important they were, but I think I can honestly say I never really entertained a single doubt. I had the most positive attitude, the most self-confidence I'd had in a long time, and part of it was because of something that happened on tour. Over and over again our audiences showed an overwhelming preference for "our" kind of music, the big-band sound, the Champagne Style that had long been associated with us. And I began to realize that if I had put my foot down more firmly during the last year we appeared on ABC, and insisted on playing the kind of music that was right for us—then we might never have lost our show.

I think we got off the track when we encountered the massive trend toward rock and roll, and acid rock, during the late sixties. Trends are mysterious. They seem to come from nowhere, and they are often very hard to withstand—or to understand! It was always hard for me, for example, to understand the fad for patched-up jeans. When I was a boy I *had* to wear them, much to my shame and embarrassment, and one of my earliest ambitions was to own a brand-new suit of clothes all my own. It was difficult for me to understand why any youngster would deliberately choose to wear old clothes, or go without a haircut or decent shoes. I've seen a lot of trends come and go in my time, and I've managed to live through all of them, from coonskin coats to leather jackets, and wide ties to thin ties—(and back again)—and of course, through all kinds of musical fads. But none of them hit us with the impact of rock and roll. I didn't like it and neither did our audience, but a great many musicians did—especially the good ones—and some of our kids began to react to it, too. My brass wanted to play higher, the guitars to twang louder, the singers to scream a little. I tried to hold the line, but I was outnumbered about forty-five to one and I didn't always succeed. Every week one or two of the singers would bring me a new song, smiling hopefully, asking to sing it, pointing out that it was Number One on Cashbox or Variety or Billboard. I used to look at those lists of top twenty or forty songs of the day and never recognize a single title. Sometimes, of course, some very beautiful new songs would come along, like "Close to You," a lovely song, a classic, one that will be around for a long, long time, I'm sure, and I was happy to do it. But even there I had a problem, because *all* the kids wanted to sing it! By the time the fifth or sixth singer had asked if he could sing it, I knew I was in trouble, and I'd have some hurt feelings on my hands if I arbitrarily assigned it to just one singer. Finally, I asked George to figure out an arrangement in which each one could sing a couple of bars. Jim laughed when he heard of my solution. "That's worthy of Solomon!" he chuckled.

If that was a problem . . . it was a pleasant one. But we had the really serious and never-ending question of how to handle the flood of new music on the market, and too many times I allowed myself to be swayed into playing it against my better judgment. I'm not blaming any of my people for this situation. Far from it. I'm blaming myself.

I should have learned my lesson the year before when we went on tour and I made my first entrance dressed as a hippie, while Ralna and Tanya and Arthur and Jack led the rest of the kids in a rock and roll number. We all looked pretty wild—especially me! Rose Weiss had designed a sleeveless bearskin jacket over a bright green flowered shirt for me to wear, and I'd added little glasses on the end of my nose, hippie beads, and a long black wig that flowed down over my shoulders. The act went over quite well at Harrah's in Tahoe, because the theater-restaurant there is relatively small, and everybody could recognize immediately that it was really me underneath all that hair. And when I announced after our number that that was enough for us, and we were going to stick with our own kind of music from then on, there was always a lot of easy laughter and applause. But when we toured to other parts of the country we got a totally different reaction, mainly because we always play in arenas that seat anywhere from eight to sixteen thousand people and it's almost impossible for anybody to see very clearly from that far away. The audience had no idea who those screaming girl-singers were, or who that long-haired hippie was, and I got the coldest reception I've ever gotten in my lifetime. There was a great silence while the audience sat there trying to figure out what was happening, and you could almost hear them thinking—"Well, here's another one gone wrong!" Even after I took off the wig and explained that it was just a joke, they didn't like it. They just didn't want us to be doing that, and it took a long time for them to warm up again. I should have realized right then how wrong that kind of music was for us. But I didn't, partly because I'm somewhat of a Dixieland swinger, and partly because the pressure was still on me from a lot of musicians in my Musical Family, and I wanted to please them. So I'll confess right now that I did let some of that music leak through into our band. And it was the worst mistake I ever made.

The tour in 1971 pointed this out to me very, very forcefully. Wherever we went . . . Texas, Alabama, Minnesota, Kansas, Nebraska, New York, Georgia . . . our fans told us with cheers and applause and requests that they liked "our" music, music with a heart, a beat, music you could remember and hum, that brought back memories. I made up my mind that we would use only that kind of music in our new syndicated series, and as soon as I got home I talked to Jim and George about it. Both of them agreed with me completely, and I called another meeting to tell the kids.

I explained exactly how I felt and why I thought we should concentrate on our own style. "I think," I concluded, "that . . . like the nation . . . we just got out of balance last year, and went too far in the wrong direction. We've just got to get back to what we do best. And we can do it, too, if you'll help me." I paused. "If you'll just not put any pressure on me to do the wrong kind of songs . . . and let me have the final say-so for the next few months . . . well, then I promise you the highest ratings we've ever had in our lifetime." Every one of them agreed to go along with me. They would have agreed to almost anything at that point, they were so highly motivated to assure the success of the show. We were completely in accord.

As we arranged to do the previous spring, we re-sumed taping again at ABC studios in Hollywood, renting the same facilities we had used for years. A few people thought I might feel bitter or unhappy about returning there. But I never felt that way at all. Why should I? ABC took a chance on us when nobody else did, and they gave us sixteen wonderful years. How could I forget that? I was happy to be back there, even after I discovered I had been assigned a new dressing room about as big as a box. The girls, too, were quartered in a new and smaller room, but none of us cared about that. It was just unimportant compared to what we wanted to do. When we arrived that first morning we found almost all the old technical and stage crew on hand to meet us. It was heartwarming for me, especially when white-haired Bobby Quy, the propmaster who had been with us since the very first show, rushed forward to give me a bear hug, his round, kind face beaming with pleasure. Bobby is my pal, bringing me a pillow for a quick nap, or handing me my baton for the show. Ten minutes after we were back in the studio, it seemed as if we'd never been away.

When I think of that first show, it seems to have a haze of blue around it. Not because we were blue or unhappy, but because we had decided to feature "No, No, Nanette" as the heart of the first hour and all the costumes were done in blue and white. And Jim and art director Chuck Koon had designed pale blue chiffon swags that were looped across the top of the stage setting on either side of the crystal chandeliers, and all the fellows wore harmonizing blue band jackets and white flannel pants. The first show had some special touches. George composed a new overture for us, a four-note trumpet introduction that held a lot of excitement, and our announcer, Bob Warren, brought us on with "The Lawrence Welk Network presents the Lawrence Welk Show!" Everything moved flawlessly. We had been presenting the songs from "No, No, Nanette" on the road and the kids had it down to a high level of perfection. Little Mary Lou Metzger was our Nanette, with her flirty, bright little voice. Guy and Ralna sang "I Confess to the Breeze," and Norma and Jim led the whole group singing "Tea for Two," after which everybody did a tap dance. When I saw the first rehearsal for this number at the Palladium, I thought Jack Imel had had a stroke of genius. The idea of the whole company doing a tap dance in unison seemed to me a terrific way to finish the show, and I was pleased to see all the kids working so hard to learn a time step. But when I saw the finished production at Tahoe, I almost called it off! Watching Joe Feeney struggle with the time step, I wondered what had ever possessed Jack Imel to think he could make dancers out of all these singers—Joe, for one, was never going to give Arthur or Bobby any competition! Nevertheless, there was something kind of charming about the sight of all the kids earnestly tapping away together, and the audience seemed to love it. The entire premier television show had a kind of sheen and sparkle to it. Everything glowed—the kids, the music, the chandeliers, the lights, the floor. Even the audience looked prettier than usual! I was extremely satisfied with everything.

But when the first Neilsen reports came in I had a momentary flash of panic, because the ratings were quite low . . . six million, two hundred thousand families. That was not too far off Matty Rosenhaus' and Ed Kletter's estimate of seven and a half million, the figure which they said should be "quite comfortable." But it was certainly not comfortable for me. I had promised the kids a big jump in the ratings, and I set out to do it.

First and foremost, of course, we worked on the show itself all the time. I asked Jim to give me more closeups. Jim is a true artist. He does exceptional work with the lighting and design of the show, and some of his camera shots are just so beautiful they should be framed, so I always hesitate to infringe on his artistic territory, so to speak. But I wanted to establish a warmer, more personal relationship between the kids and our viewers, and I felt the close-ups would help a great deal. And, of course, I went down to the wire regularly with George over the music, but that was an old story. He'd bring the sound up, I'd bring it down. He'd add more brass, I'd take it out. George is a genius and I know it. But I also had my stubborn German heart set on absolutely clear and understandable music. So we wrangled on. But the differences between the three of us were really the kind that sparked us into better results. We differed just enough to bring out the best in each other.

In addition to improving the show, we stepped up our publicity releases, so that people would know we were back on the air. Actually, we had never left it. Our contract with ABC had provided that there were a certain number of reruns they could use during the summer and they had continued to present those all summer long, right up into September. So when we made our first broadcast, on September 9, 1971, there was no break at all. We have been on the air continuously every week nationally since July 2, 1955. Our publicity chief, Les Kaufman, emphasized this point when he sent out weekly newsletters and photographs to all the media and set up telephone interviews for me. All of this helped. But we all knew that everything depended on the show itself.

I put the ratings out of my mind for a few weeks in October because I had another important event happening in my life. My first book, my autobiography, *Wunnerful, Wunnerful!* was released. The young lady who helped me write the book, Bernice McGeehan, and I had been working on it for almost two years. Bernice lives about twenty minutes away from me in the Valley, and since I was always so busy during the day, she'd usually come over at night to our hilltop house in Pacific Palisades. There was also a great deal of telephoning back and forth between us as our work progressed. I used to love it when either of Bernice's children answered the phone. Her daughter, Mary Kate, has the brightest, friendliest voice I've ever heard, outside of our own Julie Jobe at the office, and it made me feel better just to hear that happy voice on the phone. And her young son, Patrick, is one of the nicest boys I've ever known. On one occasion when we drove to Escondido, I took Patrick along and we toured the Western White House at San Clemente. He ran a hand over the shiny dark green of the Presidential helicopter and looked up at me with dazzled eyes, and I told him that maybe he could be President some day. With young people, I like to set their sights high. Who knows—maybe he will be.

Bernice and I usually worked in our music room from about seven-thirty to eleven-thirty a couple of nights a week. It's a good place to work. There are books lining one wall from floor to ceiling, a stereo, a television set, a Thomas organ, comfortable chairs, and lamps—and a distracting view of the Santa Monica city lights and the Pacific Ocean just beyond. Sometimes Bernice brought a tape recorder along to get the rhythm of my speech, or so she said (and here I thought all along I couldn't talk at all), but most of the time she just sat and took notes and listened, while I talked and talked and talked. In fact, I talked so much I got myself into trouble. Along about ten or eleven o'clock on some of those nights, I would notice an increasing hoarseness. Sometimes it got so bad I would have to stop talking entirely. I was concerned about it—downright scared—because I knew through my previous work with the Cancer Foundation that persistent hoarseness can be a symptom of an extremely serious condition. So I worried about it—and my family worried, too, as I learned one night when Donna called me. She and I have always been "pals."

Even when she was just a little girl, we seemed to have an unusual rapport, and this night was no exception. After awhile she said, "Dad—you and I have always had such a wonderful relationship—wouldn't you say so?"

"Oh, yes I would, Donna," I said warmly. "It's just been so wonderful."

"And in all those years I don't believe I've ever asked you to do me a favor—have I?"

"Uh . . . well, no, I don't think you have," I said, laughing a little. "Why? What do you want now?"

"Nothing for myself, Dad. But if I ask you to do something for me . . . do you think you would do it?"

"Well," I said, "I don't know about that. What is it you want me to do?"

"Promise you'll do it first," she insisted.

I couldn't imagine what she had in mind. But I thought about all the years she used to wait for me when I was out on the road, the way she used to fly into my arms when I came home, then tuck me in bed for a nap, tip-toeing out . . . "so Daddy can get a little rest" . . . and I knew I would do just about anything for her. "Okay, Donna," I said. "I promise. Spill it!"

"Well, Dad," she said quietly, "I want you to go and see two different throat specialists, and find out exactly what's wrong with your voice. Please, Dad, it's important to all of us."

I was jarred. I hadn't expected that at all, and I must confess that like most of us, I wasn't any too anxious to go to the doctor. But I knew she was right so I said, "Well, I think I can do that, Donna. I promise I'll do it right away." Things were made a little easier for me because both Donna and Shirley are married to doctors and they gave me a list of top specialists. I selected two and made appointments to see them. Each doctor poked and prodded and took tests and

X rays, and each told me to come back in a few days for the results.

I don't know when I've awaited the outcome of diagnostic tests with more worry than I did then. I've had a number of medical tests over the years, but none that concerned me like this one did. Finally the day came for my reports, and I was tremendously relieved when the first doctor told me he could find nothing seriously wrong.

"In my opinion," he said, "you just have a sensitive throat, and you need to give it more rest." I was so delighted at this wonderful news that I didn't really comprehend what he was saying. But the second doctor put it a little more bluntly.

"Sit down, Mr. Welk," he said when I walked into his office. "I think we've discovered your trouble." My heart sank. I thought he had found something the other doctor had overlooked.

"Oh?" I said, trying to sound brave. "What is it?"

He leaned across his desk and looked directly at me. "Your problem is," he said flatly, "you talk too much. My advice to you is drink lots of water—and keep your mouth shut."

I've tried very hard to follow his advice ever since, and the drinking water part is easy, considering that that's the only drinking I do anyway. But the not-talking part is quite difficult. I love people and I love a good conversation, and just working in the office or on the show requires a good deal of talk during the day. But I've learned to pace myself and rest my voice frequently, and I've had very little trouble since. At the time, I simply cut down the length of each working session on the book, and within a matter of days the problem had righted itself.

I wanted very much to do a thoroughly honest and complete life story of my own. There had been a few other books written on my life, and some of them had been inaccurate, so I wanted to clear up any misconceptions. I was astonished at the kind of memories and feelings you can dredge up when you begin to look down the long years of your life. I began remembering people and events I hadn't thought about in years. Sometimes I would burst out laughing . . . but other times I found myself close to tears as I recalled some half-forgotten incident out of my childhood. It was a very moving experience for me, but the thing that impressed me most of all was the realization that the principles on which I had based my life, really worked. There had been many times over the years when I had asked myself whether those standards weren't just too tough, whether I wasn't asking too much of myself, or others. But those bedrock values, rooted in the Christian training I had received in my earliest youth, really did work. I loved working on my book! It was very satisfying to me to see it take shape and express the things I felt so deeply about. We finished it just before the cancellation by ABC, but the events of that momentous month forced us to rewrite the last chapter a little, and Prentice-Hall brought it out officially in October. I was so pleased with it that I agreed to plug it on a book tour. I'm not sorry I did . . . for one thing, it landed on the Best Seller list where it stayed for several months, a fact that made Bernice very happy, and me, too, as a matter of fact. But, of course, the tour, in addition to the rigors of the show, was quite a workout.

I traveled with Bob Howland, the West Coast representative for Prentice-Hall, and I made appearances in thirty-nine different cities, on TV shows or in department or bookstores. I could never have done it without Bob's expert help. Like Lon, he also had the knack of getting me in and out of places with great ease, making the tour a pleasure. I especially enjoyed going to the bookstores. I'd sit at a table while people lined up for autographs, and I always tried to write something personal in each of the books. It took a long time to do it that way, but it meant a lot to me. If our fans cared enough about us and our show to buy a book, then I wanted to say something personal to them. And it really tickled me when more and more young people showed up in the line. I'd look up and see a pretty young thing standing in line and automatically I'd say, "Is this for your mother?—Or your grandmother?"

But more and more one of these girls would surprise me by saying, "No. It's for me. I watch your show all the time myself."

I think the Madison Square Garden show and my book tour marked a real turning point for me. From that time on, we have had a steadily increasing audience of young people. And I love it!

We had a lot of fun on our book tours. I made the rounds of the Johnny Carson show, Merv Griffin, Dick Cavett, all the major talk shows, and I got a kick out of putting them on the spot. On the Carson show I talked Johnny into doing a stiff-legged polka, and it turned out his dancing wasn't much better than my talking. On the David Frost show I played the accordion while Pearl Bailey sang. That was a great thrill for me. I had always thought of her as one of the great ladies in our business, and even though we'd had no chance to rehearse beforehand, she was just so sensational we couldn't seem to do anything wrong. At one point she told the audience that her mother was a great fan of ours. "Why, one time I called Mama long distance clear across the country," she related, "and I said . . . 'Well, hello, Mama, this is Pearlie Mae!' . . . and Mama said, 'Pearlie Mae, don't bother me, I'm listening to Lawrence Welk!' . . . and hung up!" I thoroughly enjoyed that show and also What's My Line. The directors were convinced I could never fool the panel with my accent, but I pitched my voice down very low, to a Larry Hooper basso profundo, and did manage to fool them. At least for a little while.

I didn't make the whole thirty-nine-city tour in one fell swoop. Bob and I would fly out and do a few appearances and then fly back home so I could do the show, then back out again. And I included book appearances during our road tour with Lon wherever I could, too. It was hard work but I felt it really paid off for me the day I was on the Mike Douglas show in Philadelphia. I had made arrangements to leave before the show was over, because I had to catch a plane for Orlando, Florida, and Walt Disney's wonderful Disney World. After I finished my segment, I made my exit and raced for the car that was waiting outside. Just as I got to the door, someone grabbed me by the shoulder and pulled me back a little.

"Wait a minute, you've got a very important telephone call," they told me.

"I can't take it," I panted, "I have to go, I'll be late for the plane."

"You better take *this* one," came the reply. "It's from your publishers and they say it's vital!" I took the call. And it was Bill Eastman from Prentice-Hall calling to say we had just landed in the Number Eight position on *The New York Times* Best-Seller list, one of the most important in the nation. What a thrill! I nearly flew to Florida under my own power, I was brought so high, and I couldn't wait to tell Bernice. It was the first major book for either one of us, so it was a double thrill. I really couldn't believe it. Here I was, a man who had never finished the fourth grade—a man who still has trouble spelling—and yet somehow, I had managed to write a book that appeared on the Best-Seller list.

All during this time I was working very hard on the show. The kids took me at my word and did not pressure me a bit about doing songs they preferred. And the production board chose a perfectly acceptable group of songs for each week's show. Nevertheless I had problems. Every Tuesday I'd arrive at the studio at ten o'clock, full of smiles, hopeful, eager to get going, sure that this was going to be the best show we'd ever done. But week after week, by eleven o'clock I was down in the depths. It was nobody's fault really. It was just that we were all working so hard to make the show as perfect as possible and yet somehow, there always seemed to be at least one song that wasn't prepared quite right or didn't have the flow I wanted. So week after week I'd start re-rehearsing, changing, adding, moving around, substituting. It was exhaustive and difficult work, and I didn't want to blame anybody, because I frequently have trouble explaining exactly what I mean (I've had that trouble all my life), so I thought maybe I simply hadn't gotten my points across clearly. It's nearly impossible for me to explain exactly why I feel a song is right or wrong anyway. I just seem to know in my bones when it's right, but I can't tell you why. It's just instinctive with me. At any rate, those first few weeks were very tough. Maybe it was because we were over-anxious, trying too hard, I don't know. I just know it was exhausting.

Sometimes I would get so tired, so wrung out by show-time that I was literally shaking with fatigue, and I would think, well, I just can't go on, I can't do it. But when I got dressed and walked out on stage—the magic was there, always there. The moment I came out for my pre-show chat with the audience, my nerves would calm right down, and I'd begin to enjoy the show. And by the time it was over and everything went well—as it always did, somehow—I was feeling fine again. I'd drive home happily, the tiredness slowly evaporating as I drove through the bright lights of Hollywood, out onto the freeway over Beverly Hills and up into my own Pacific Palisades hills. By that time I was fully relaxed, completely confident—and full of plans for the next week's show.

Our first Neilsen report had covered the week ending September 12. We received a weekly report from Neilsen rather than a single-performance report because our show played on different nights in different parts of the country. Most places it was on Saturday night just as usual, but in some cities it aired on Sunday, and occasionally on Thursday or Friday. So it necessitated a comprehensive weekly summary. That first report on September 12 was the one that had disappointed me so, with its rating of six million, two hundred twenty thousand. Less than a month later, on October 3, 1973, we received our fourth report. This one read—*ten* million, two hundred and fifty thousand! I had expected a healthy increase, but an increase of four million was almost unbelievable. We were all absolutely delighted! There were congratulations, smiles, happy laughter. Ten million families translated roughly into some thirty-six million viewers, and that's a pretty good rating. I felt again how fortunate we were to have such a wonderful, loyal audience. We had put our whole hearts and souls into this venture. And I felt now that the kids and I were on the right track at last.

13

My "Kids"

PEOPLE OFTEN ASK me where I find the members of our Musical Family. Well, I've found them just about everywhere . . . in ballrooms, county fairs, hotel lobbies. Most of our members came to us through the regular method of auditioning, either by sending in a tape to us or performing in person, but I always keep my eyes open every moment, because you never know where you'll find talent. I was on a tour in behalf of the Cancer Fund in 1968, when I found Clay Hart performing in a hotel nightclub lounge in Charleston, West Virginia. After hearing one number, I didn't even ask him to audition for our production board—I just hired him on the spot. I discovered Sandi and Salli when they competed with two hundred other young singers at a mass audition at the Palladium in Hollywood, and that's a day I won't soon forget. I thought they were by far the best of the group and I invited them down to the studio the next day to sing again. But even though I was drawn to them, there was something about their material I didn't exactly like. It was just too far-out. I had Frank Scott take them to the rehearsal room and work out a very simple arrangement of "I'm Gonna Sit Right Down and Write Myself a Letter," and ten minutes later they were back to sing it with such fresh, breezy authority I hired them right away, too. Gail Farrell tagged in on me at a dance at the Palladium one night and fast-talked herself into auditioning, in front of the entire Palladium audience. Mary Lou Metzger simply telephoned and asked for an audition while she was in Los Angeles appearing on the College Bowl show. Cissy was really discovered by Bobby, and Tanya was brought to our attention by Mary Lee Schaefer, the president of our Fan Club. Norma was already a well-known singer in Hollywood musical circles when we more or less invited her to be on the show. I found Anacani, our first Mexican singer, at Escondido, or rather she found me. She and her family had come to our restaurant to find out how she could go about auditioning for our show and I just happened to be there. She stopped me just as I was leaving the restaurant, and we went back inside and she sang for me then and there. I wasn't too sure about the songs she was singing—they were all in Spanish—so I asked her to learn a couple I would recognize like "Cieleto Lindo," and come back in a couple of days. She did, and sang for the people who live in our Country Club Retirement Village, and she got so much applause from them that I said, "Well! If you folks like her so much . . . I guess I'll have to put her on the show!" She promptly burst into tears, and as I looked around the room I could see that she wasn't the only one.

"Why, you're crying!" I said in surprise to one lady who was dabbing her eyes. "And you . . . and you!" It seemed as if the audience was just as touched and delighted as Anacani and her mother, and I must say, they were right. Ana has been a real asset to the show. She is also the Singing Hostess for our restaurant at Escondido, sharing honors with our tall baritone, Tom Netherton. I first found Tom in Bismarck, North Dakota, when some friends of mine, the Harold Schaefers, told me about him and said they felt he might be perfect for the show. I was impressed when I met him. He was one of the most handsome young fellows I'd ever seen, and he had a personality to match. He has the niceness, the warmth, the admirable "quality" of character we always associate with Norma among the girls. When he sang, he had a big Robert Goulet-type voice, and I liked him enough to invite him out for an appearance on the show. As luck would have it, the stagehands were on strike when he arrived, and there was no show for him to go on. So, I had him sing for our board who were absolutely bowled over by him. We signed him immediately and arranged for him to become the Singing Host at Escondido as well. The same day we invited Tom out to appear, we had also invited a little nineteen year-old country singer named Ava Barber. She sang for the production staff and they were so taken by her performance that I hired her, too. I had met her originally because she had mailed a tape to Jim. He played it for me and I liked it so much I wrote and told her that if she ever got to Hollywood we'd be glad to listen to her. Not long after that, I had the pleasure of going to Nashville for a Music City Golf Tournament, and our little friend was ready and waiting for me in the clubhouse at the golf course when I arrived. I sat down at the piano in the lounge and tried to accompany her while she sang a few songs. I didn't recognize any of them, however, so finally I said, "Do you know 'I Never Promised You a Rose Garden'?"

"Sure," she said, and after just one chorus I knew I had another winner and I invited her to appear on the show, too. Immediately her husband, a young man named Roger Sullivan, said quickly, "Mr. Welk, I play the drums. Could I audition for you?"

"Oh, my," I said, "I'm sorry, I'm going to tee off in just a few minutes, we wouldn't have time to get your drums out here."

"Oh, no problem," he said, grinning a fast Irish grin. "I've got them right here!" Saying which he reached in his pocket, got out a tape recorder and flipped on a tape of his drumming prowess! He was good, too.

So I never know where I'm going to find my people, nor do I know when I'm going to find them. Joe Feeney was brought to my attention originally by a priest who wrote me about his wonderful talent. Ken Delo auditioned through Sam Lutz, as did Arthur Duncan. Both of them, interestingly enough, had worked in television in Australia a few years previously. Henry Cuesta, our brilliant clarinet virtuoso, was playing in Toronto, Canada, with his own band when he was heard by the famous jazz trumpet man, Bobby Hackett. Bobby immediately suggested that Henry get in touch with our George Thow, who used to be with Tommy Dorsey's band in the old days, and see if he couldn't audition for us. George advised Henry to mail us a tape of his playing. He did, we listened—and hired him, in a hurry! I took Henry and our equally talented pianist, Bob Ralston, with me to Nashville, Tennessee, in March of 1974, where we made our debut with the Nashville Symphony, which was a great thrill for us all. I found Bob, by the way, when he was a fifteen-year-old piano soloist and won a contest which I had helped judge. I'd forgotten about that when we hired him fresh from Freddy Martin's orchestra. Jimmy Roberts and Dick Dale were both from other orchestras, as was our outstanding jazz trombonist, Bob Havens. Most of the fellows in my band worked with other top-flight groups previously, and several of them learned their craft in NORAD, the North American Air Defense Band. Johnny Zell, Don Staples, Dave Edwards, and Richard Maloof all perfected their techniques there, and I would like to say thanks right now for the good training they received. Myron Floren, whom I hired in 1950, came to us over the loud objections of Bill Karzas, the manager of the Trianon Ballroom where we were then playing. "Welk!" he exploded, "one accordion player is bad enough, but two? Besides, they tell me this Floren fellow plays better than you do!" Well, of *course* he played better than I did . . . that's why I hired him. I never stop trying to improve.

I had a girl singer one time who told one of the fellows in the band that as long as she was with us, no other girl singer would ever set foot on our stage. I happened to overhear her and said, "Just a minute. Please don't tell me our band wll never get any better than it is now." I didn't mean she wasn't a good singer. She was. But if one girl singer is good, two might be better, and three delightful. You have to be open to change all the time.

I seem to have a reputation for conservatism and stability and I believe that's true. But that doesn't mean we don't change. We may change slowly, but we do change. Years ago I had just one singer, then two, then a quartet. Today we have soloists, trios, choral groups, dancers, jazz combos—you name it and we've got it—and we try constantly to improve the sound of our music.

I'm not a creative kind of musical director in the sense that I come up with something entirely fresh and unusual. I think my usefulness lies in evaluating somebody else's ideas and adapting them. Jim continually spouts over with creativity, for example, and I feel it's my job to consider what he comes up with and adapt it into our framework. Same way with George.

In some ways I guess I'm more of a salesman than anything else. You can see that, readily enough, every time I introduce one of the people on our show. When I say that they're wonderful or they did a great job, or they have pure, sweet voices, I really mean that. I think of myself as a salesman, too, but when people say, "Oh, Welk can sell anything," I'll have to disagree with them. I can't sell a talent or a personality if there isn't talent there to begin with. But if I believe in someone, I'll do everything in my power to help him (or her) succeed.

That includes helping them overcome little habits which could be potentially harmful to them. Along this line, we've had a few cases of tardiness, which almost seems to be an occupational hazard with some of the folks in our profession. A few years ago we had one musician who was really wonderful except he had a terrible habit of arriving late for practically every rehearsal, with the result that we sat around and waited while production costs mounted. Naturally I wasn't too thrilled about this, so I spoke to him about it from time to time and he kept promising to do better but never did. That summer the problem became even greater because we went up to Harrah's to play an engagement, and of course, Harrah's policy has always been to present their productions as if they were on television or radio, with everything timed right down to the last minute—including a ten-minute countdown. We were instructed by the management that the curtain would rise precisely at eight-fifteen, and that if any member of the orchestra was not on stage and in his chair at the moment the curtain rose, he was not to come out on stage during the performance. I delivered this message to the fellows at a band meeting prior to our first performance. Immediately, the latecomer's hand shot up into the air. "Yes?" I said. "What is it?"

"Mr. Welk," he said briskly, "suppose I *am* a little late some night? What should I do?"

"Just as I told you," I replied. "Don't come out on the stage. Wait in the wings till the show is over."

"Oh," he said, sounding slightly baffled. "All right. But . . . *then* what should I do?"

"Then," I told him gently, "you walk downstairs to my dressing room, sit down, and wait for the management team. And then we'll have a conference with them—and find out if you're still with the band!"

That was enough to keep him on time for the next few nights, but sure enough, on the fifth night he was late again. With less than thirty seconds to spare, he came screeching up to the backstage entrance in a cab, jumped out—dragging his heavy musical instrument case behind him—and huffing and puffing, went tearing down the long sloping ramp toward the stage. Halfway down he could hear the stage manager begin intoning the countdown over the intercom system: "Ten, nine, eight, seven, six . . ." Panic-stricken, he raced the rest of the way down and, just as the announcer said . . . "three, two, one, YOU'RE ON!" . . . he rounded the corner, took one huge flying leap and landed on stage and in his chair! He had made it with less than a second to spare.

One of our pretty and talented girls had a problem, too, showing up late quite often for rehearsals, and holding up production every time. I talked to her, Jim talked to her, Myron talked to her, and she smiled and promised to do better every time. But every week or so, she was late again. Finally in desperation, the production staff took matters out of my hands entirely and told her that, as a reminder to help her do better, they would do the show without her the following week. She promptly burst into cries of protest and when the producers were unyielding, she came down to see me about it. She tried everything . . . smiling prettily, looking sad, giving me dozens of explanations, and—when all else failed—tears! (Like everyone else on the show, she had heard I'm a soft touch for tears, which is true, but by now I've experienced more than my share of "shedding" and it's not as hard for me to resist as it used to be.) I tried to explain to her that we were only trying to help her overcome her habit, which was making things difficult for everyone, and we weren't trying to be unkind. "This is really a last resort," I said. "We just don't know what else to do. And tell me, young lady . . . if you were in

my place, what would *you* do? What would you
do if one of your best performers was late week after
week, holding everybody else up? Now, why don't
you just be a good soldier and take your medicine?"

The only answer was loud sniffling and aggrieved
looks. But gradually the sobs subsided and a small
grin appeared in its place. "Well," she said, looking
penitent, "I think maybe I can remember to be on
time from now on, Mr. Welk!" And she has.

I've had people stop me in hotel lobbies, airport
lounges, and I even auditioned one fellow—a whis-
tler—in the men's room! I try always to keep my
eyes and ears and mind open, so I don't overlook talent, no matter in what unlikely place it seems to crop
up. What I look for, almost more than talent, is quality, character, a particular attitude that seems right.
And if I immediately like the person a lot chances
are the audience will like them, too. Nevertheless,
I've had differences of opinion with my production
staff from time to time. Several years ago I hired
one of our singers over the unanimous disapproval
of everybody else. Something told me that this singer
had great potential, however, so I went ahead with
my plans. (I'm not going to tell you which singer
it is . . . after all I do have *some* secrets!) . . . but
this particular performer has turned out to be one
of our most enduring and popular ones. On the other
hand, I've made my share of mistakes. The ones that
hurt most are when the people we've tried so hard
to groom and help, just walk away. But that's part
of life and I accept it. I've had, and still have, the
most wonderful, loyal group of talented performers
anybody could have had. I love them all.

14
Hawaiian Polka

AT NINE O'CLOCK in the morning, January 1, 1972,
I sat in the back seat of an open convertible, waving
and smiling at the million and a half people who
stood bundled against the bright blue morning chill
of the Pasadena New Year's Rose Bowl Parade. Beside
me sat Fern, waving also, just as thrilled and delighted
as I was. Our two eldest grandsons, Robbie, son
of Shirley and Bob, and Jimmy, eldest child of Donna
and Jim, rode with us, almost overcome with excitement. Being asked to be Grand Marshal of the Rose
Parade was an honor that meant a great, great deal
to me, and even Fern, who generally begs off big
public appearances, was more than willing to accept
this one. She got together with Rose Weiss before
the big day, and the two of them picked out a suit
for me in dark lavender and pinkish tones, to contrast
with Fern's purple outfit, complete with a purple hat
and an ostrich feather that curled round under her
chin. And as we drove down Colorado Boulevard
between the jampacked, whistling, cheering, shouting
throngs, the sun shone, the breezes blew—and Fern's
ostrich feather tickled her chin! I knew she was
unusually excited that day because she had managed
to misplace her jewelry—and for Fern that's really
something. We had spent the previous night at the
Huntington Hotel as guests of the Parade Committee,
so we'd be on hand for the six o'clock breakfast and
parade lineup. That meant getting up at five in the
morning in order to get dressed and, in addition to
getting herself ready, Fern wanted to make sure Robbie

and Jimmy were groomed to the teeth, too. In all the excitement she forgot to put on her rings, which she had removed the night before and placed in a glass dish on the dresser. She didn't even miss them until we were walking into the festive luncheon after the Parade. Then she suddenly clutched me by the arm and whispered urgently, "Lawrence, I left my rings in the hotel room . . . and I'm afraid I left the door open, too!" I turned a little pale myself, as I made some fast excuses and dashed off to call the hotel manager. On the way, I couldn't help grinning a little. If any would-be burglars had hoped to make a big haul from the Welks, they were probably crying with disappointment by now, because Fern's jewelry is not exactly what you'd expect! She is still wearing the slender platinum wedding band with little chip diamonds, and a matching engagement ring with one big diamond in the center, that I bought for her in 1931. That was the best I could do in those days. In fact, it took every penny I had, but I wasn't worried because I confidently expected that Fern, who was a registered nurse, would have saved up a tidy nest egg to see us through our honeymoon, if necessary. To my chagrin, it turned out she had a grand total of about ten dollars, and I had to call on my good friend Tom Archer to bail us out. In later years things got much better for us and I could have bought Fern a much more impressive set of rings, but she never wanted me to. So I was relieved when the hotel manager assured me that the maid had found them and turned them in.

"It's okay, Fern," I whispered, sliding back into the chair beside her at the luncheon table. "Your rings are in the hotel safe. But . . . please try to be more careful in the future, won't you?" She just gave me a look, because *I'm* the one who's always losing jewelry.

Just a few months earlier I had lost an extremely

valuable watch given to me by Bill Harrah. It was a really beautiful, oblong-shaped wristwatch, made of finest brushed platinum, edged with diamonds. In fact, it was so gorgeous I decided to wear it on special occasions only, and I put it away for safekeeping. The only trouble was, I forgot where I put it! (I think I should warn you younger readers that this is one of the hazards of life you have to look forward to. You just don't remember things very well when you get to be my age.) For weeks after that—well, for months really—I looked for that watch. It had been losing a few seconds of time, so I thought maybe I had taken it in to the jewelers to be adjusted, but when I called, the jeweler said, "No, Mr. Welk, I'm sorry, but you didn't bring it in here." I called Sam Lutz to see if he had it. I probably called Don, too, and I looked everywhere. I went through the pockets of every suit-coat I owned at least twice, searched all my luggage, my dresser drawers, the car, everywhere I could think of. Finally I had to admit defeat, and in desperation I confessed the whole thing to Fern and asked her to intercede on my behalf with St. Anthony, the patron saint of lost articles. I could have asked him myself, of course, but Fern is famous in our family for her strong connections with the good saint, and I figured in a case as severe as mine, I'd better go right to the top.

"Well," she said, doubtfully, "I don't know. The last couple of times I've asked him, I haven't been too successful. But—I'll try."

A few mornings later, as she tells it, she was making my bed when she got to thinking about my lost watch. She stopped in the middle of smoothing the blanket, looked up to the heavens, and addressed her friend directly. "St Anthony," she said firmly, "you know how much I believe in you. But you just haven't done a thing for me lately! Lawrence has lost his wristwatch and can't find it anywhere. I know you can't do anything if it's not here in the house—but if it is . . . won't you please lead me to it?" Then she went back to making the bed.

"A few minutes later," she reported, "I felt an overwhelming impulse to go look in your clothes closet. I opened the double doors and there on the floor were some shoe boxes, and a fancy box that looked like a miniature pool table, wrapped in a plastic cover sheet." (It was a jewelry box given to me by Ralph Portner, public relations man for the Palladium.) "Well," continued Fern, "I took off the plastic wrapping, opened up the lid of the box . . . and there was your watch!"

She didn't tell me all this right away. Fern has her own little way of teasing, so even though she found it early one morning, she didn't tell me a thing about it all day. But that night at dinner I wondered why she had such a cat-who-swallowed-the-canary look on her face, and why she kept waving her left arm in the air. And then I saw it, glittering on her wrist. "My watch!" I gasped. "Where did you find it, where was it?"

"Oh," she said, airily, holding out her arm and inspecting the watch, "it was right where you left it, in that fancy jewelry box in your closet. You really should have asked me a lot sooner," she added complacently. "I knew St. Anthony wouldn't let me down."

I nodded, thoroughly impressed. I always did think Fern had a hot line to St. Anthony and now I was absolutely convinced. I decided in the future to go to her immediately. It would save a lot of time.

By February of that year I began to relax a little. The ratings were up, our morale was up, everything seemed to be going quite well. Syndication, I discovered, had certain advantages networks didn't have. Performers are not under the domination or whims or caprices of anyone—except the public. If the public likes you, you can stay. You don't have to deal with a middleman . . . (or his wife) . . . who may or may not like you. You can deal directly with your own fans and I liked that, I liked it very much. There was a kind of security in it based on the one thing I feel is most important of all—personal integrity. As long as we produced the best show of which we were capable, and tried constantly to please our audience, I felt that we could stay on the air just about as long as we wished. The "kids" would be taken care of, their future made secure. The thought made me very happy, because the single most compelling reason I had tried to go on after our cancellation, was to try and take care of my Musical Family. And I felt now, that if they continued to work with such dedication, I could step aside one day soon and let them carry on without me. Nobody knew better than I, that I wouldn't be around for ever to direct things, and I have always wanted so much for them to be able to take over some day. The way things were going, those early months in 1972, I felt we were fast approaching the stage when they'd be able to do so. Things moved without friction. Ideas for new shows seemed to spring without letup, not only from Jim and Jack, but from all the kids. Even George simplified the music to a point where I stopped grousing at him! Everything was just "wunnerful" and in March, when we went off on another tour with Lon, it was almost a repeat of our tour the year before, perfection all the way. This time Lon booked us into cities and areas which we had not played the year before. As a rule he schedules our appearances approximately two to three years apart, so we won't wear out our welcome. Our welcome was tremendous wherever we went. At one show we had a ninety-nine-year-old man ask to come up on stage and dance the polka with Cissy. At his age, I was almost afraid to let him do it, but he did such a beautiful job I felt like a kid again myself. If he could dance that well at ninety-nine, then I had years of good living left ahead of me. I asked the old gentleman if he could tell me his secret for such a long and healthy life. "Sure," he said. "Just keep breathing!" Good advice.

When we played near Carbondale, New York, where my old friends John and Margaret Malone live, I spent part of one day with them, and what a wonderful experience that was. Carbondale is a small-ish town, and after school all the children followed me around like the Pied Piper, and I loved it. Signing autographs for children is very different from signing for adults, I discovered. The little ones chat so openly with you, as you sign the back of their gum wrappers or lunch sacks or whatever, and there is something so moving about those fresh, young, innocent faces. Later on that same day John took me to St. Joseph's Hospital where I visited with the patients. It was a good day.

I was full of unusual vitality all during that tour, but then touring often brings on a resurgence of energy in me. In fact, it sometimes seems that the longer I go without sleep, the more wide-awake I become—as some of those who were with me when I played at the New Jersey Garden State Art Center can remember all too well. The Art Center is located in Holmdel, New Jersey, and it is one of the most beautiful places I've ever seen. It's an outdoor amphitheater set into the side of a grassy green hillside under a floating circular roof which is supported by slender white colonnades—a sort of super outdoor-pavilion, designed by the famous architect, Edward Durrell Stone. All the seats are of red leather, and the contrast of the white buildings and the red seats and the green lawns and trees is really spectacular. We opened the New Jersey summer season of symphonies and popular-music concerts, and it was a gala formal affair with Governor William T. Cahill as honorary chairman. All the ladies were in lovely summery evening gowns and the men in tuxedos. Afterward, there was a party given by the sponsors of the event, and it was almost four o'clock Sunday morning before John Malone, who had driven Lon and Bernice and me up from New York, got us back to the hotel. By that time I was more than willing to go to bed and get a little sleep before our nine A.M. takeoff at La Guardia Airport. But I had reckoned without John Malone, who moved in and saved my spiritual health for the day.

"Now, let's see, Lawrence," he said, studying a schedule as we pulled up to the hotel, "there's a church just three blocks from here, so I'll pick all of you up in an hour, and we can make five-thirty Mass and go directly out to the airport." He beamed, as if the problem were all solved.

"Uh . . . well, John," I said, stalling a little, "that's wonderful, but really—you don't have to do that. You know . . . I think . . . uh . . . when you're traveling, the church gives you a dispensation . . ."

"Oh, sure, I know all about that," said John, disposing of the whole matter in one sentence, "but I also know how strongly you feel about it, Lawrence . . . so don't worry about a thing! I'll be here to get you to Mass on time." Well—I know when I've been finessed!

"Okay," I said heartily, "that'll be wonderful, John, thanks very much. We'll be ready." Both Lon and Bernice looked a little stricken at this, because that meant they'd have to get up at five o'clock, too. And I can't say I was too thrilled. But John was right. It's very easy to get a dispensation from your churchly duties these days, but it's not necessarily the best idea. I've felt all my life that making a thing difficult makes it more worthy, far more blessed, and I was really grateful to John. So we all went to our respective rooms, and bright and early—well, early anyway—at five o'clock, Lon and I knocked on Bernice's door to find that she was up and dressed, but that was about it. She was still half asleep. John, however, waiting in the deserted lobby downstairs, was bright-eyed and fresh-faced, eager to go. He walked us briskly through the early morning Sunday hush (it was strange to see the New York streets so deserted) and into St. John the Baptist Church. At five-thirty in the morning we were almost the only worshippers there, but if the priest was startled to see our little group, he made no sign. He preached a full-length sermon and said a lovely Mass, his quiet voice on the altar echoing through the small, dark nave of the church, reminding me of the early morning masses in Strasburg. I reflected that no matter where you go, you find that same kind of reverence in churches everywhere; but somehow, in the very early hours of the morning, it seems even more powerful.

By the time the service was over and we were on our way to La Guardia, I had had less than one hour's sleep and I should have been exhausted, but I wasn't at all. In fact, I was feeling just fine, and at the airport I had a quick breakfast of tea and rolls and then went around chatting brightly with all the kids, some of whom were looking a little wan and pale in the early morning light. We were scheduled to fly to Memphis for an afternoon performance, and then back to Los Angeles, and nearly everybody was anxious to get home. Everybody but me! I was still feeling so good I was ready for another week's tour as I kept telling everyone.

"Lawrence," said Bernice a little desperately at one point, "aren't you tired?"

"No," I said, honestly. "Not a bit. I guess I'm a freak." I was really wound up that morning, and as we flew along I talked and talked to Lon and Bernice about our training program. I thought I was speaking very brilliantly, too, coming up with one unusual idea after another, really selling my plan, and I couldn't understand why one or both of them weren't making any admiring comments. I took a closer look. Both of them were sound asleep. I sighed, and took a little nap myself.

The ratings held up all during February and March, dipped slightly to nine million, five hundred thousand in April, and then went back up to ten and a half million where they remained. Encouraged, we began making final plans for our first big location trip out of the continental United States. In July, we flew to Hawaii, all forty-five of us. With wives and husbands and children, plus technicians and directors, that made a group of one hundred and fourteen. It was quite a caravan, and it all got started because I play golf.

Art Kelly, president of Western Airlines, is a golfing pal of mine at Bel Air Country Club and one day he and I got to talking about the fact that Lawrence Welk Champagne Music and the Champagne Flight of Western would make quite a team. The upshot was that we decided to fly to Hawaii for a special show, with Western providing the transportation. Mason Mallory, head of sales for Western, did a superb job handling the details, and in the process he and I became good friends. In fact, he provided us with one of the songs for the show, a number he composed himself, called "In Hawaii." (He and his wife, Ruth, provided us with more than that, incidentally. They became good friends with Gail Farrell during that trip, and later on Gail met their handsome young son, Rick, and before the year was out the two of them were married!)

None of us knew that that was going to happen when we flew to Hawaii though. Fern came along on that trip—for Hawaii she broke a long-standing rule about road trips—and she and I sat up front in the VIP section as the Western plane took off from International Airport. But I couldn't stand such luxury, and five minutes after we were airborne, I was circulating through the rest of the plane visiting with the kids and other passengers, while Fern read a book. Tanya and Larry had brought along their babies, "Buns" and Kevin, and nearly all the boys brought their wives and older children, too. There was such a holiday mood aboard the plane I wondered if we could settle down long enough to do a show. At the airport, the Lieutenant Governor, George Ariyoshi, was there to meet us along with the Hawaiian Royal Guards and some very beautiful girls from the Aloha Week Court, who draped such quantities of leis around our necks that we could hardly see over the top. But the thing I remember most is not the leis or the pretty girls or even the kisses. It was the giant-sized Hawaiian man who did his own version of the hula for us. He was dressed in a short, flowered costume that showed plenty of his mid-section, and everybody cheered as both his costume and his tummy waved in the breeze. Maybe you saw the picture. It was widely reprinted all over the United States, and is included in the picture insert of this book.

Mason had checked us into the Waikiki Hilton, a lovely hotel built right on the sands, where Fern and I had a beautiful suite. She took a little nap as soon as we arrived, so I decided to take a little swim. I descended to the hotel pool, dove in and swam the length. That was the last pool swim I got all the time we were there. When I surfaced at the other end, I found crowds of friendly fans, all holding out autograph books or postcards or cocktail napkins for me to sign. I soon discovered that signing soggy pieces of paper is not as easy as it might seem. I also discovered that if I really wanted to swim, I'd better sneak down to the beach and jump in the ocean, which I did frequently all the time we were there.

I also had a little trouble getting through the hotel lobby, and one day, when Governor John Burns invited me to play golf with him, I realized I had a little problem on my hands. I had to figure out some way to get through the lobby quickly when his car arrived; otherwise I'd be late, and you just can't be late for the Governor of Hawaii. I finally solved the whole thing by pulling my golf cap down over my ears and then hiding behind my golf bag as I crept stealthily out to the car. It worked just fine.

One night Mason and Ruth and a group of us went to the home of Axel Anderson, the composer of many wonderful songs, the famous, lovely "Hula Hands" among them. His wife, Peggy, had set the dining table outside on the patio, amid rocks and giant ferns and Hawaiian ti leaves, so it seemed as if we were inside a beautiful grotto. Later, we went inside to the high, vaulted living room, built in the traditional Hawaiian style, and had an old-fashioned musical evening. Axel played the ukulele, Peggy sang, and I played some old German folk songs with my version of an Hawaiian beat. Even though we were on an island in the middle of the Pacific, three thousand miles from home, I felt as if I were back in Strasburg again. There was something about the warm family feeling, the way we took turns entertaining, and then wound things up with a mass rendition of "Let Me Call You Sweetheart" that reminded me very much of our musical evenings at home.

Everywhere we went on the Islands, we ran into fans, too, which also made us feel at home. I guess it's safe to say I've had my picture taken in every state in the Union and a good many places in Europe, too, but I don't think I've ever been "shot" as many times as I was in Hawaii. It was click, click, snap, snap, wherever we went. Most of the time it was fellow tourists rather than the Hawaiians themselves. There was even one group of Japanese fans who jumped out of their tour bus and lined up politely for autographs. I was amazed that they even knew us. I thought at first maybe they had heard us on recordings but it turned out they had seen us on television. It was a wonderful feeling to reach across a supposed barrier of distance and language, and shake hands with people who suddenly seemed like old friends.

We worked hard every day on the production sketches which Jim had lined up during an earlier location trip, and he had everything running smooth as silk. I remember one shot in particular in which Gail and Dick Dale rode to the top of the Ilikai Hotel in an outdoor elevator which showed a panoramic view of the city and sea below, and another in which the kids skimmed over the clear, clean ocean waters in a catamaran, their hair blowing wildly in the wind. I was proud of our girls in those scenes. Even without any makeup, and in the bright Hawaiian sunlight, they looked beautiful.

We ended the week with a mammoth personal appearance show in the HIC auditorium in Honolulu which Lon arranged for us. It happened to be Norma Zimmer's birthday, so the audience stood and sang "Happy Birthday" to her. She was very touched, and, watching her as she stood in the spotlight, an orchid in her hair, looking so lovely with tears shining in her eyes, I could feel my eyes begin to fill up, too.

It was that kind of trip all the way, close, warm, loving. Partly it was because we were all together, having family fun. But partly it was Hawaii itself.

Hawaii has a mood, a feeling all its own. In some ways it's the perfect representation of all the rest of our United States. There are all kinds of races and religions living together in the most perfect harmony. There was a complete absence of any kind of tension between different races. It was a wonderful feeling, one I could relate to right away, because I have never been troubled with any kind of racial or religious bigotry at all. Our own show is composed of people of almost every religion you can name and every kind of racial background, too, a kind of Little America, so too speak. I've always enjoyed it and felt it gave our program a richness nothing else could.

Hawaii reinforced that feeling a thousand times over. We saw brown Japanese and Hawaiian faces, and the lighter, more strongly-boned ones that were a mixture of Hawaiian and Portuguese and American Yankee, some of the most interesting and beautiful faces we'd ever seen. And there was music wherever we went, too, that soft, pervading Hawaiian music that seems to come right out of the trees and the clouds and the breeze. Hawaii was a mixture of friendly people and magnificent weather, music and good conversation, wonderful golf and swimming. It was a high spot in a series of high spots in our travels around the nation, such a perfect experience in every way that I kept thinking about it as we flew home. In fact, it sparked me so much I got my yellow note pad and began busily writing out some brand-new plans.

To go to Alaska.

15

Trouble in the Family

MAYBE THINGS WERE too good. I don't know. But after the Hawaiian trip, we coasted for a while. I should have known how dangerous that can be, but we had added a few more stations to our network and the ratings were holding up so well I guess we were lulled into security. I began playing a little more golf and catching up on the reading I love, and I just wasn't on top of the show the way I usually am. The result was, we were in deep trouble almost before we knew it. When I realized what was happening, it was the most profoundly disturbing discovery of my lifetime. I discovered that what the networks and other forces had been unable to do to us—we were doing to ourselves. We were losing our own show.

I noticed it first in little ways. One of the kids would be a few minutes late to rehearsal . . . and the next week, they'd be a little later. Or one or two of the singers would forget the lyrics to a song and make up their own as they went along. This kind of goof can get by on stage sometimes, but not on television which magnifies every mistake mercilessly, and I was a little upset by it. But I was even more upset when one of the kids suggested we use cue cards every week so we wouldn't have to memorize the songs at all.

"Oh, no," I said firmly, "not that! You know how I feel about live songs." To my mind there is just no comparison between the quality of a live performance, and one in which you record your songs ahead of time and then just stand there and mouth the words to the music. Some of the natural fire and spontaneity is lost when you do that. So when you see our singers with their neck muscles a little strained, and real expression in their eyes, it's because they really are singing, right then.

Other little things bothered me. I'd see groups of kids standing around in corners yawning, waiting till the last minute to rehearse their numbers, instead of working on them as they usually did, or else sitting out in the darkened studio dozing until their turn came up. They seemed to be drifting along in a strange kind of apathy, so deep that the whole tone of our performance began to drop. As if in answer, our ratings showed a slight drop, too.

I was disturbed about it and talked frequently with Jim and George. "Well, I wouldn't worry too much about the singers forgetting their lyrics," said Jim reassuringly one day. "That doesn't happen too often. It's probably just a summer slump, Lawrence, they'll be okay."

And as we got ready for our upcoming Tahoe show, I thought Jim was right. In the excitement of rehearsals, the kids seemed to get their old enthusiasm back. Once in Tahoe, however, we were in worse shape than before, and in addition, a lot of little things that had never bothered us previously suddenly loomed up as terribly important—the size or order of billing, for example, or the fact that the dressing room doors were kept locked . . . or unlocked! Alarm bells rang in my head. I had been through situations like this before, in which one person or one incident had magnified things out of all proportion, so that it threatened to bring down a whole company, and I tried to stem the tide of resentment that seemed to be rising.

But on opening night, I realized just how far things had gotten out of hand. We made the usual number of cuts and changes after the show, something that had never upset any of the kids before. But this time

it did. A couple of them came to me with real hurt
in their voices and told me thay'd rather have their
numbers taken out entirely than have them shortened.
"I've put too much into that song to have it cut down,"
one said almost tearfully.

I could certainly sympathize with their feelings
and told them so, but I also pointed out the problem
we faced of fitting a certain number of songs into
an allotted space of time. I added that a show that
moved quickly and brightly was usually much better
than one that was over-long, and everyone seemed
to understand this completely. On the surface then,
it appeared that everything was fine—but I have a
sharp ear for discords—and I knew it really wasn't.

Things came to a head toward the end of the second
week, when the chorus muffed our big closing number
badly, and instead of being upset about it, they treated
it as a joke. I could hear them laughing as they ran
downstairs after the performance, mimicking what
they had just done. That made me mad clear through!
One thing I will not tolerate is a sloppy performance,
and I called a meeting the next night just before the
show, in my dressing room.

Everybody filed in and settled down on sofas and
chairs or sat on the floor, boys immaculate in their
opening-act costumes, girls all made up and looking
so pretty, so sweet, and so young I very nearly called
the whole thing off. But I realized there was a basic,
very important principle at stake, so I plunged
ahead.

"Boys and girls," I said, looking around the room
at all the faces I loved so much, "something happened
last night during our performance that I just don't
think is right. It's not so much that you didn't do
the song well . . . it's that you didn't seem to care.
Now I know some of you have been unhappy with
the cuts and changes we've had to make and I can
sympathize with you. But I'm afraid you've overlooked

something very important." I looked around the room again. "We're not in this business to see who gets to sing the most solos. We're in it to put on the best possible show we can . . . every night." I paused. "I'm sure you've all seen the long lines of people waiting to get in to see us. Well, I should think instead of squealing about every little thing, we would all be on our knees every night thanking God we still *have* audiences like that! We should be doing everything we can to please them." I stopped and then added quietly. "A few months ago—we didn't have a show at all. Now—we do. Let's not lose it for each other."

The girls all crowded around me then, with little hugs and tearful kisses, promising to do better, and the men agreed also. And things did go better for a while after that. But human nature is human nature, and back in the safe confines of the studio, turning out a show regularly week after week, some of the company fell right back into their old habit of complacency, of taking things for granted.

I was at my wit's end as to how to combat this feeling, and I held almost daily conferences with Jim and George. We talked about the problem at length, and one day as we parted, I added, "And by the way, Jim, please give me some more closeups, will you?"

"More?" he asked in surprise. "You must be kidding!"

"No. No I'm not," I said. "I not only want more—I want them bigger."

"If I make them any bigger they'll go right off the screen," protested Jim.

"That's okay," I said, stubbornly. "I want them just as large as you can make them, and I want you to hold them for quite a while, too . . . at least eight to sixteen bars in each song."

"Okay," said Jim, a little skeptically. "We'll give it a try!"

I talked with George then. "See if you can't help me kindle that spark in our people again, George," I urged. "It's important, vital to our success."

"I know," said George. "But Lawrence, the greatest majority in the group are working up to their top level now. It's only a few who aren't."

"Well, then, get through to them! It only takes one or two people to pull down a whole show, George, you know that. And I want simpler music, too," I added. "Clean and bright and . . . and understandable, the kind we built our reputation on."

George flushed, insulted. "It *is* simple," he cried. "It's clean and simple right now!"

"Okay," I said, grinning a little at his outburst. "Okay. Just make it a little more simple, that's all!"

George snorted and walked off, muttering about the inconsistencies of German bandleaders. I knew both he and Jim had the best interests of the orchestra at heart just as much as I, and I wasn't at all concerned over the differences between us as to taste and judgment. Things like that had always been easily worked out. But I *was* concerned . . . terribly concerned . . . about the sudden attitude of disinterest in the band, the loss of communication. Something was keeping the orchestra from doing its best work. They just didn't seem to care anymore.

I could have issued orders and demanded the kind of behavior from them I wanted. But that wouldn't have brought about their real cooperation . . . and I couldn't have done that anyway because it goes against my deepest nature. I have always had a respect for the rights and talents of others, and I have always had a horror of being the kind of person who orders others around. I saw too much of that sort of thing in my early years on the farm in North Dakota, where I sometimes saw neighboring farmers treat their help and even their own families with such cruelty that they made their lives unbearable. Later on, I saw the same kind of behavior in a few ballroom and theater managers who ruled their small domains like dictators. It was so unpleasant I vowed I would never do anything like that, and I used to literally pray that I wouldn't fall into that kind of behavior. I have tried all my life to lead my orchestra through persuasion and suggestion. In spite of that, however, I have somehow built up a reputation as a very stern taskmaster. To this day, whenever a new reporter or writer interviews me he will hymn and hum around for a while and finally ask: "Are you really as tough as they say?" This baffles me completely! I think I've gotten that reputation partly because I'm of German descent, and Germans are famous for their dictatorial tendencies, and partly because I believe so strongly in self-discipline. But that's the point. I believe in *self*-discipline, not the kind that is imposed on you. I rarely make demands. I just don't believe in it. Now, however, circumstances were shaping up so that I was being forced into making them.

Something else was pushing me, too. If I lived to be a thousand, I could never adequately express my appreciation to Matty Rosenhaus for his faith in me. He had come through at a time when we were just about as low as we could get. He had offered a helping hand when nobody else had, and I was passionately grateful to him. I had promised him a show with the highest rating we were capable of getting, and I knew that if we went on the way we were going, we could never live up to that promise. I wasn't about to let him down. Matty deserved the very best, and I was determined to give it to him.

Now that I look back, I think perhaps I should have taken a much sterner stand, and taken it much sooner than I did. I perhaps didn't make myself clear enough, because I was hoping that things would work themselves out without any pressure from me. As it was, I didn't begin to exert any real pressure until the day the orchestra came in for rehearsal and sat through an entire number (I think it was "Maybe," which seems appropriate!), and just pretended to play it. Obviously they had pre-recorded it and they were sitting in place, "lip-synching" in time to the music. A couple of the fellows weren't even bothering to do that, and they were "playing" their horns without moving their lips! It looked ludicrous on the monitor of the TV screen in my backstage office and I grabbed the phone and called Jim in the production booth upstairs.

"Jim . . ." I began—

"I know, I know!" he said hastily. "I saw that, too. The band pre-recorded that number, Lawrence. They said they didn't have time to learn it for the show."

Before I could say anything else, George came bursting in with his hand up to forestall any arguments from me. "Lawrence, I know you don't want anything but live numbers on the show, but this was a special situation. Let me tell you about it."

He went on to say that when the band had met the day before for rehearsal and pre-production tapings, several of the fellows told him they didn't know the number well enough to play it live and they wanted to pre-record it. "I didn't want that because I feel exactly the same way you do about live performances, but . . . well, yesterday was a killer, tremendous pressures all day long and the guys wore me down. Kenny Trimble more or less represented the fellows and he's taken responsibility for the whole thing."

As if on cue, Kenny came in and agreed with George. "That's right, Lawrence," he said. "We didn't think we knew the number well enough to play it live."

I suddenly felt very, very weary. "Kenny," I said *"why* didn't you know that number? You fellows have been playing it off and on for years. And if you didn't know it when it was assigned for this show, then you should have told me about it sooner so we could have substituted something else. It seems to me you fellows are not giving it the care and concern you should. How can I get that across to you? If we don't give our show every bit of talent and energy we have every week, then we're just not going to have a show!"

Kenny nodded, his face very serious. "Boss," he said, "it won't happen again, believe me."

We tried to salvage the number by putting sheet music on the floor at the fellows' feet, but that looked even worse. If you think it looks funny for an orchestra to sit on a bandstand and pretend to play, you should see one trying to play while sneaking peeks at music lying on the floor. It just doesn't work, and after watching this spectacle for awhile, I sighed and said, "Well, boys, it's just not coming off. Let's take it out."

We substituted a vocal, and that disturbed me, too, because we were still receiving hundreds of letters every week asking us to increase the number of band instrumentals, and cut down on the vocals. And yet here I was, with the best group of musicians I'd ever had in my life, unable to answer those requests—because the boys hadn't bothered to learn their music. I talked to them again, pointing out that we had to play our best every single week, not just when we felt like it. "We can't let down even for a minute, boys," I told them. "If we do, we're done for!"

All of them agreed with me, and all of them promised to do a better job. And yet . . . to my anguish . . . in the three weeks that followed, they played so far below their usual standard, I was forced to cut out every one of their featured numbers.

Something had to be done. I thought about it night and day, tossing and turning all night long, unable to sleep, trying to figure out what had happened to us. I finally decided that when we had been faced with a genuine crisis—when we had been in danger of losing our show entirely—we had worked with the best talents we possessed. But now that we had passed the crisis, everyone had let down, and was simply taking things for granted. It may have been a standard reaction to stress . . . but that didn't make it right. And I realized, as I spent one sleepless night after another, that much as I loved my Musical Family and wanted to keep their jobs for them, I would not . . . and could not . . . keep on with a show in which we were giving less than our best. It was not fair, to either our audiences or our sponsors. It was not even morally right in my opinion, and so, reluctantly, I came to a very sobering decision. And I called a meeting of my production board to tell them about it.

We all gathered as usual in my office—George, Jim, Ted Lennon, Lois, Jack Imel, George Thow, Joe Rizzo, Myron Floren, Curt Ramsey. Lois bustled around offering coffee before we got down to work, and then I stood up and began to talk.

"Gentlemen," I said, "you must know by now that something is very wrong with our organization. I've tried, over the past few weeks, to point this out to you. I've asked for changes, for simpler music . . ."

"Lawrence," cried George, in exasperation, "will you stop bugging me about the music? It *is* simple, it's simple right now!"

"It isn't simple enough!" I said, so sharply that everyone was stunned into silence momentarily. "But that's not the real problem, and you fellows know it. The real problem is the performance and morale of the band as a whole. Now I'm not going to belabor you with the fact that our audiences have been asking for more and more big-band music, and we haven't been able to give it to them for three weeks running.

And I'm not going to point out all the little ways our performances have slipped, because you know about that as well as I do. But I *am* going to tell you this." I stopped, and looked slowly around the room at their silent faces. "If we can't do a better job than we've been doing—I will give up the show completely. I would rather do one or two good specials a year—than a second-rate show every week."

George leaped to his feet and he was so wounded that tears spouted from his eyes. "How can you say that, Lawrence!" he shouted. "We've worked our tails off for you . . . I've worked around the clock for twenty-five years for you! And here you are telling me . . . telling all of us that we're not doing acceptable work!"

His voice cracked, and in the angry discussion that followed, most of the men backed up his viewpoint completely, their voices rising, too, until finally Jim, speaking with that grace under pressure which he usually manages to display, said evenly, "Lawrence, I think it's fair to say that every person in this room has given—and is giving—his best efforts to the show."

"That may be," I said doggedly, "but we're not getting through to our kids! Let me just say this to you. Ten years ago I turned over the bulk of production to you folks so you could learn the business. The dream of my life is to be able to turn it over to you completely some day—so you'll have something when I'm gone. But I can't do it, if things go on like this! It just wouldn't be right! And, gentlemen," I added, suddenly overcome with weariness, "at almost seventy years of age, I'm not about to start in all over again. I'll throw in the towel first."

There wasn't a sound. After a moment I turned and walked swiftly out the door and down the hall toward the elevator, close to tears. As always, when I am in the grip of extreme emotion, I wanted to be alone.

I felt terrible. In the heat of excitement generated in our session—a session which had lasted almost three hours, I noticed now to my surprise—George had threatened to quit. Whitefaced and trembling, he had leaped to his feet and cried, "Okay, Lawrence, I've had it! When this season is finished, I'm leaving. I'm through!"

At the moment I didn't know whether George, or anyone else for that matter, was still with me. I knew they felt I had questioned their talents, their reliability. But I had not. I was challenging the level of our total performance as a musical family. It was something I could no longer accept.

Life is funny. When my band walked out on me in the thirties, I was convinced nothing worse could ever happen to me. And nothing did, until we lost our show in 1971. I was convinced then, that that was the lowest point of my life. But both those failures had been set off, to some extent, by other factors. Other people, other forces had caused them to happen. But this . . . this was different! This we had done to ourselves, and I was heartsick just thinking about it. If I have ever been at any real crossroads in my life—that was the time. I loved my kids like my own and I wanted to do what was best for them. Nevertheless, I was ready to give up the show completely. If we couldn't do it right—then we just wouldn't do it.

Driving home from the office, I debated about telling Fern the whole story, but in the end I decided against it. No reason to upset her. And then again, one of the things I've learned over the years, is that problems often have a way of working themselves out so it's unnecessary to talk about them. But that was a long, long evening! I worked on a magazine article for a couple of hours but finally gave up and wandered aimlessly around the house, trying to get tired enough to sleep. I stood at our den windows for a while and looked out at the lights of Santa Monica twinkling below, and I could see the tall white oblong of our new office building glistening in the moonlight. We had all been so proud and happy about that—but I wondered now if the spirit which had helped us build it was beyond recovery. Finally I went in and lay down on my bed, but I couldn't sleep, and I wasn't at all startled when the phone suddenly shrilled about twelve-thirty in the morning.

"Lawrence?" said a voice, cautiously. "Listen . . . I hope I didn't disturb you . . . but I can't sleep." It was one of the men who had been at the meeting.

"That's all right," I told him ruefully. "I can't sleep either."

He cleared his throat. "I . . . uh . . . listen, Lawrence, I've been thinking and I believe we've been doing an okay job . . . an adequate job, you understand . . . but we haven't been doing the *best* job we could. And so I . . . uh . . . oh heck," he floundered, "I just wanted to say you are absolutely right—and I for one, will be doing a much better job from now on!"

That made me feel so much better I turned right over and went to sleep! Even so, the days that followed were pretty difficult. We had our dramatic meeting just before a two-week "vacation"—a lay-off in our regular schedule of taping, so I had no real way of knowing what was happening. I had a few encouraging telephone calls during that time, but I knew nothing at all for sure, and I spent a lot of time playing golf, going to our home in Palm Springs, driving down to Escondido, reading, praying.

When the two weeks were up, Lois and I drove across town from Santa Monica to Hollywood for our weekly taping, and I was conscious of my stomach jumping. I had a really bad case of stage fright because I just didn't know what I'd find. Maybe I had angered the whole "family" so much we'd never get our old spirit back.

But the minute I walked in the door . . . I knew we were all right. Everybody was there, and everybody was smiling, smiling with a look that said, "Listen, boss, we understand, and we're not going to let down anymore." All the singers knew their songs. All the sketches were well-rehearsed. And the band? Ah, the band played like they used to play, all out, full of melody and fire, right on top, all the way! It was a wonderful feeling, one of the best I've ever experienced.

Nevertheless, I was still cautious. This might be just an over-reaction, a one-shot show that was spectacularly good, and what I was after was not just one good show, but a constant weekly string of them. So I waited to see how things would work out. Next week the band sounded even better, and none of the numbers had to be cut. I learned that Jim and George had talked to the fellows and each of the sections had gotten together on their own—the horns, strings, and so forth—for extra practice. And I was pleased to hear more practice tootles coming from various dressing rooms during the afternoon. The closeups were the best we'd ever had, too, and I got on the phone immediately after the camera rehearsal to tell Jim so.

"That last closeup of Tanya was beautiful," I cried. "Just beautiful!"

"Really?" he said somewhat drily. "You didn't think it was a little *too* close? You can see her tonsils!"

"Doesn't matter," I assured him. "Her tonsils are beautiful, too!"

The whole show began to move ahead with a kind of pace and surging excitement we hadn't had for a long time. The music was crisper and cleaner, the performances beautifully controlled . . . even the costumes looked prettier! The next set of ratings we received seemed to confirm my feelings, because they began moving up again. (And as I write these words, we have passed the thirteen million mark, which translates into over thirty-five million viewers.)

But best of all, we had our "family" back again. All the petty little complaints simply vanished, once the kids understood we were in danger of losing our show. It was a little like the person who never realizes how sweet life is, until illness threatens him with the loss of it. If he recovers, he finds the greatest pleasure in simplest things, in the fact of just being alive. So it was with us. When our kids finally realized we might lose our show and our wonderful loyal audience, their attitude changed completely and they began to work as never before. Practice became a joy, rehearsal became a joy, performing the greatest joy of all. And the unhappy experience that threatened to tear us all apart brought us closer together than ever.

I was deeply happy about that. Nobody knew better than I what a tremendous chance I'd taken by talking so strongly to my people. I might have alienated them all. But I didn't . . . because they cared just as much as I did. That's what saved us, the fact that we all cared so much. I would never have spoken out as strongly as I did if I hadn't cared, and they would never have reacted with such heat if they hadn't cared, too. We may not always agree on the *way* to reach our goals. But we are solidly together in our care and concern for each other as we work to achieve them. And that means more to me than almost anything in the world.

I worried for a while over whether to tell this story in this book or not. It would be so easy to just gloss over things and present all of us as faultless men and women who never get mad or unhappy or jealous or lazy. But that wouldn't be honest, because we're not like that. We're human, too, and we have our feelings and our failings just like everybody else . . . maybe more so! I do believe our people are the finest in the world, a cut above the average, and I'm very proud of them. But that's not to say that we don't have our faults . . . and that certainly includes me. But we do try hard to correct them.

None of the kids ever came and told me they would do a better job. They just *did* a better job.

And George never came and told me he would stay, either. He just stayed . . . and I think I felt we were pretty well back to normal the day he blew up just as usual and stormed out of my office muttering about my lack of talents as a musician. Listening to him out on stage shouting at the fellows just the way he always had, I grinned happily. George's screams of anguish, more than anything else, told me we were back in tune again.

16

Seventy

In March I celebrated my seventieth birthday. It was a kind of a shock to realize I was seventy years old. I had never been shy about broadcasting my age, mainly because when I was in my fifties, I had been so ill I was afraid I'd never make it into my sixties. When I did, I was so happy and grateful over my continued good health that I've been absolutely delighted to tell my age ever since, no matter how old I get. Still, there's something rather disconcerting about turning seventy. It was made a lot less painful for me when Fern and I walked into the Beverly Hills Hotel Crystal Room one night, and right into a surprise party. It really was a surprise, because it was two weeks before my actual birthday. Matty Rosenhaus had called me from Florida and told me he had to fly to the Coast on business and hoped Fern and I would be able to join him for dinner. Of course we were very happy to do so, and on the appointed night Matty, Don, Sam, and Fern and I walked downstairs at the hotel to a private dining room. Just at the foot of the stairs, however, Don and his wife, Yvonne, gently turned us around and steered us into the ornate Crystal Room and there . . . seated at twenty round tables centered with roses and crystal . . . were some two hundred of my closest and dearest friends. They all rose to their feet and sang "Happy Birthday" as we entered, and then applauded as Fern and I waltzed around the room.

After the beautiful dinner, Jack Minor walked up to the microphone to emcee a show the kids had put together, and he immediately got roars of laughter by announcing that, in the Minor household, in addition to their regular evening prayers, they now read one chapter of *Wunnerful, Wunnerful!* every night. Kenny Trimble made a rambling, funny speech on behalf of the boys in the band, the kids sang "North Dakota" with some very special, hilarious lyrics, and Matty made such a moving speech that both he and I were in tears.

But the most wonderful moment of all came when I was standing at the microphone alone, wondering what would happen next. In the sudden hush that followed, I saw a tall, thin, bespectacled man walk slowly across the polished dance floor toward me. I peered closer . . . and then ran out onto the floor and threw my arms around him, almost overcome with emotion. It was our dear Larry Hooper. Larry had undergone open-heart surgery three years before, and then suffered an almost unbelievable series of complications, including one full year when he had been unable to speak at all, because of scar tissue that had formed in and around his vocal cords. There was no assurance that he would ever talk again, and on two occasions we had despaired of his very life. But somehow, hoping against hope, we kept him a member of our Family, praying that somehow, he would recover.

Now, there he was, looking exceptionally fit and smiling broadly, as if he had a secret to share. And he did. When we got back to the microphone he began to talk . . . and the words rolled out in those familiar, deep bass "Hooper" tones.

"Lawrence," he said, after the initial wave of applause had subsided, "I guess you know this is almost a miracle. But . . . Beverly and I never gave up. We knew, with the help of the Man Upstairs and all of you here in the band, that somehow, I would make it. And I guess I have. The doctors tell me I can

come back on the show next fall. And Boss, . . ."
he was smiling, smiling with his heart, "Boss . . .
I can sing again!"

The house came down. What a birthday present!
The best I could possibly receive. True to his words,
Larry did come back the following September, as
you know if you've seen the show, and if anything,
his voice is richer and fuller than ever. What a great
blessing for us all.

We left for our spring tour just a few days after my
birthday party, with Lon doing his usual expert job
of guiding us, and we had wonderful crowds from
coast to coast. In almost every city they sang "Happy
Birthday" to me, and I thought, well, if I have to
turn seventy, this is certainly the most pleasant way
to do it. And to my great satisfaction, the kids continued to work with such tremendous initiative and enthusiasm, both during the tour and on our return home,
that I felt entirely comfortable about taking frequent
time off to make appearances on behalf of the Cancer
Foundation, along with my charming co-chairman,
country music-comedienne Minnie Pearl. She or I
flew all over the country during 1973 for rallies
and kickoff luncheons, and I thoroughly enjoyed it.
That wasn't the case in 1968, the first year I served
as chairman. I was so scared that time I thought
I'd never make it.

I had to accept the chairmanship in the first place
because Ed Kletter had more or less talked me into
it. He and Matty Rosenhaus had long been associated
with the work of the Cancer Foundation so I knew
what a tremendous job it had been doing, and I wanted
very much to help. But I also knew that being chairman
entailed making a lot of speeches to campaign workers
around the country, and the thought of standing up
before a thousand people at a banquet and delivering
a speech was almost more than I could take. "Oh,
Ed," I said, "I want to help—but can't I just play

the accordion? You know how terrible I am at making speeches! I . . . I just can't do it!"

"Oh, sure you can," said Ed, heartily, with that easy confidence that somehow makes you feel you can do almost anything. "Nothing to it. I'll tell you what, Lawrence," he added. "I'll come along with you for the first few appearances, and do most of the talking. Now, believe me, you won't have to worry about a thing."

He finally convinced me to accept and, true to his word, he met me for the big kickoff luncheon in Cleveland, Ohio. We got together beforehand in my hotel room, and Ed sat down to help me with the speech I had written. He rewrote it a little, and then rehearsed me. I stood up in front of him, and self-consciously read the entire speech, complete with stiff little gestures. "Great, Lawrence!" he cried with enthusiasm when I finished. "Wonderful, terrific! Now—do it one more time." I did. "That's just great," he said, beaming, "absolutely wonderful! Lawrence, you'll be sensational!" Then he took my speech and tore it in two.

"What are you *doing?*" I asked, aghast. "That's my speech you just tore up!"

"Oh, you won't need it," he assured me. "You've got it all in your head, you just talk off the cuff."

We finally compromised by writing notes on cards to which I referred through my little talk, and I don't think I've ever been so scared in my life. I sat in a panic all through lunch waiting to be introduced, and when I heard Ed announce my name I swallowed hard, pushed back my chair, and stumbled up to the microphone. Then I fainted—well, no, not really, but I was close to it, and I really believe that if I hadn't been holding on to Ed on one side and the microphone on the other, I would have gone right down on my knees. As it was, my legs were so shaky I looked as if I were standing in a strong breeze.

It wasn't that I wasn't used to speaking to large groups of people, but never to one like this, composed of doctors and scientists and other brilliant leaders in the fields of research and economics. I kept thinking miserably to myself, what in the world am *I* doing here? But somehow I lurched on through my speech while the audience sat in sympathetic silence waiting for me to finish. When I did, they gave me a huge round of applause, whether from relief or approval I didn't know (but I have a pretty good idea!). I was afraid I'd never get up the courage to make another speech after that, but somehow I did, and as time went on I got so I actually enjoyed making them. I think the secret to making any speech is to care so much about what you're talking about that you forget about yourself and your jumpy stomach. And of course I cared . . . and care . . . very much about the wonderful work the Cancer Foundation is doing.

We had lots of fun on some of those appearances. In Rapid City, South Dakota, I attended a breakfast rally for campaign workers, and a very pretty young lady came up to tell me she had watched our show since she was two years old. "I'm twenty-two now," she said, "and I have a two-year-old daughter of my own, and now *she* watches your show." I thought her story was so charming that at a big civic luncheon later that day, I asked her if she'd mind coming up and telling it to the folks. Reluctantly she did, but when she got up to the dais she took one look at the assembled throng, and burst into tears. "Oh, Mr. Welk," she wailed, "you didn't tell me I would have to come up *here!*"

"Oh, now, please don't cry," I said, putting an arm around her. "I didn't want to upset you, I just thought the folks would like to hear your story, it's so cute." And in an effort to make her feel more comfortable, I kissed her. Well, that's as good a reason as any. She calmed down a little, told her story, and went off to warm applause. Immediately thereafter, I began awarding citations to campaign workers who had done an exceptionally good job. The first one up to receive an award was a sprightly little lady about eighty years old, very straight and trim. I handed her the citation and reached out to shake her hand. But she ignored it and, with a twinkle in her eye, tilted her cheek toward me, obviously asking for a kiss. I pretended not to know what she meant, so the audience began shouting . . . "Kiss her, kiss her!" . . . until I gave her a great big kiss on the cheek. Following the first lady, came a parade of eight more, and every one of them came up on the dais grinning, with their heads tilted sideways so they'd get a kiss, too. I was really beginning to enjoy this, getting almost into a rhythm of reaching behind me, picking up an award, turning and bestowing a ceremonial kiss on the recipient as I handed it over. But the ninth time I stopped short . . . because the ninth recipient was a man! He stopped short, too, and we both stood awkwardly for a moment wondering what to do next. Suddenly the gracious wife of Governor Richard Kneip of South Dakota rose from her chair, ran over to the man, pulled his head down—and kissed him, smack on top of his shiny, bald dome! Well, there was absolutely no way I could top that. While the audience screamed with laughter. I handed him his award and he bowed low, Mrs. Kneip's lipstick still shining brightly on his head. And that ended the kissing spree for the day.

We found a wonderful spirit of cooperation at all those meetings. In 1973, I made twelve such trips to all parts of the country, from California to Florida, from New York to Washington state. But I think the most outstanding jaunt of all was our trip to Hawaii. For this one, Fern unbent again, and decided to come along too. She likes Hawaii, that's obvious—but there were a few hours there when I was convinced she didn't like it at all, or else she didn't like me! At the time we made the trip, we were celebrating our forty-second wedding anniversary, so it seemed like a good chance for a second honeymoon. And as we flew in over the Islands they looked as lovely as we remembered. And again the folks in Honolulu outdid themselves with friendly courtesy, and again we were put up in an absolutely gorgeous suite at the Sheraton Waikiki. Fern was a little fatigued when we arrived, so after dinner that night she excused herself and went up to bed. I stayed on for the business on hand with the officials of the Cancer Foundation and it was after midnight when I said goodnight and went up to our suite. The door was locked, and I couldn't get it open no matter how hard I tried. Fern had evidently put the inside lock on, and no amount of fiddling around with my key could get it open. I rattled and knocked and hissed "Fern, Fern!" as loudly as I dared, and tried the key a dozen times—but nothing worked. Finally I went downstairs and called her on the house phone. It rang and rang, but no answer. Obviously she was sound asleep. In desperation I went to the desk clerk and told him my troubles and he roused out the manager who took me back upstairs and opened the door with his master key. I tiptoed across the vast living room and into our bedroom, where just as I expected, Fern was sound asleep. But one thing puzzled me. The phone on the table was right beside her bed, and I couldn't understand why she hadn't answered it. It was still bothering me when I drifted off to sleep.

Next morning, in honor of the occasion, I blew myself and ordered breakfast in our room. The waiter served it at a table in front of the floor-to-ceiling windows overlooking the sparkling sea below, with Diamond Head in the distance, outlined sharply against the clear, blue sky. As we ate, the soft ocean breeze billowed the glass curtains and carried in the scent of pikaki and Hawaiian ginger flowers, and if I'd staged the whole thing myself I could never have come up with a prettier setting. So, after breakfast, I cleared my throat and made a little speech. "Fern," I said, "as you know, this is our wedding anniversary."

She nodded.

"Well," I said, "I just want to tell you what you've meant to me all these years. You've been a . . . a wonderful wife, in every way."

She smiled, pleased.

"You've given me three fine children," I went on. "And you've always made our home such a pleasant, happy place to be." She smiled again, turning a little pink. "Fern," I added, really getting warmed up to the subject, "you've always kept everything so neat, so clean! In fact, you're the cleanest person I know!"

She was really smiling now, just beaming. "Why . . . thank you, Lawrence."

"And, Fern, you've always been so . . . well, so considerate, and loving with me."

She smiled even wider, really enjoying this whole tribute. "That's very nice."

"Fern?"

"Yes, Lawrence?"

"Why did you lock me out of our room last night?"

There was a second act to this little comedy. After we'd talked about it and had a good laugh, I said, "Fern, one thing puzzles me. When I called you from the lobby the phone rang and rang. Were you that sound asleep, you didn't hear it?"

"Oh, sure," she said matter-of-factly. "I heard it. But I just figured it would be for you anyway—so I'd let you answer it!"

We spent three lovely days on the Islands. Ed and his wife, Rae, had come with us and we spent a good deal of time with them. I have been so fortunate to

have had such fine relationships with my sponsors
over the years. Ed and Matty and I are very close,
and I've also had a wonderful relationship with the
Dodge people who sponsored us in the very beginning
and are with us again today. When I had been so
worried about finding good sponsors as we went into
syndication I kept thinking about Dodge, and on the
spur of the moment I called Bob McCurrie, vice-president of Dodge-Chrysler. "You know," I said, "you
people took a chance on me years ago when I knew
very little about television. Well, today I know a lot
more. I can express myself better than I used to.
I'm just wondering if it wouldn't be a good idea for
us to work together again. The way I feel about you,
there's nothing I'd like better."

He listened closely. "Lawrence, I like what you're
saying," he said. "Why don't you have Don get in
touch with our advertising agency?"

I did, and within a day or so Don called back,
beaming. "You'll never believe this," he crowed, "but
Dodge wants to sponsor us." I was pleased. It was
a good feeling to be doing the show for the sponsors
we respected so much.

Being seventy, I decided, didn't seem to slow me
down much. I continued to tour on behalf of the
Cancer Foundation, taped our show every week,
played in a few assorted golf tournaments, worked
on a new book (this one), and . . . flew to London.
One of our sponsors was Mutual of Omaha, headed
by my good friend, Mr. V. J. Skutt. Mutual had
originally become our sponsors in a rather unusual
fashion. When we first went into syndication, I was
aware that there were some negotiations going on
with them, so one day when I was in Washington,
D. C., I decided to call up Mr. Skutt, an old friend
of mine. I telephoned his home office in Omaha,
Nebraska, but his secretary told me he was out of

town. "However, I can give you a telephone number where you can reach him, Mr. Welk," she added . . . and then proceeded to give me the number of the Statler Hotel in Washington, where I was staying! Amused at the coincidence, I immediately called the hotel operator and discovered that V. J. was not only staying in Washington in the very same hotel I was, he was also staying in the room right next to mine! I was astounded, and needless to say he was pretty astonished himself when he opened his door and found me standing out in the hall. Mutual went on to sponsor us for several seasons, and Mr. Skutt had invited Fern and me to go to London for a big party they were hosting in honor of some of the long-time employees.

I was a little hesitant about going because I had one of my terrible colds, but it seemed to be such an important event that Fern and I finally decided to go. We stayed in London for three days, and the highlight of our trip was the Awards Banquet held in the Grand Ballroom of the Grosvenor Hotel. Fern and I sat at the head table along with David Frost and Mrs. Bob Hope, and watching the kilted Scotch bagpipers march in playing the pipes beneath the massive crystal chandeliers hanging from the gilded ceiling, I couldn't help thinking it was a long, long way from Strasburg.

The London trip was very impressive, very exciting, and so was a trip I made to Spain later that year for an International Golf Tournament. But let me say right here and now, I was absolutely delighted to get back home again. This country is the best country in the world, and I hope none of us will ever forget it.

And then I did something I never, ever expected to do. I became a "Professor," and at the University of North Dakota, no less, in Grand Forks, North Dakota.

Dr. Jerome Tweton, the chairman of the UND department of history, had been offering a five-week mini-course on the impact of our band on popular culture, and had suggested that I lecture for one day, as part of the curriculum. The idea that a college was actually teaching a course based on our music was overwhelming, but the thought of actually "teaching" was even more so, and I tried to beg off when my old friend Lloyd Stone, vice-president of the University Alumni Association, first asked me to do it.

"Well, Lawrence," he said quietly, "you have a lot of experience and information to impart to these young people. I think you should." I thought it over. I certainly couldn't talk like a real "perfessor" and I had no scholastic training whatever to back up a lecture. On the other hand, I had a great deal of experience in commercial music and television, and maybe I owed it to my young friends to tell them what I could. I decided to go ahead.

On the big day, I met first with Dr. Thomas Clifford, the good-looking president of the University. He introduced me to some of the other teachers at an informal seminar and then took me on a Cook's tour of the University. Then, a little nervous, I marched into "History 395," to meet my "students."

There they sat, at tables rising on a graduated tier of eight levels, in the semi-circular classroom. I stood at a podium and read from a prepared text for a while, but after about ten minutes I discarded it and asked for questions instead, and it was then that we got to the heart of the matter. Those young people were just so interested, so involved! They wanted to know everything about popular music and television and the best ways to get ahead, and I tried my best to answer them and get across my basic message—that the most effective way to accomplish anything is to ask the very best of yourself and never let up for a minute. I looked out at all those intent young faces, at the pretty girls with their long blonde hair falling over their shoulders, and at the young men . . . a few of whom also had long blond hair falling over their shoulders . . . and I tried to communicate what was in my heart.

We got along famously. I told them something about the history of popular music as I knew it, and played a tape of a number called "Henry's Waltz," which had been played by the Schwab brothers at a Welk family reunion in Strasburg a few weeks previously. It has such an irresistible beat that it's almost impossible to sit still when you hear it, and it's a "heavier," more countrified version of the famous Strauss Viennese waltzes. But all of that music comes from the same source. I explained my theory of what makes music popular, why I have always played music which people love to hear, rather than what my musicians or I think they *should* hear, and we wound up the class with an impromptu accordion and dance session. But the real high spot, for me, was working with the band later on.

There they sat, some seventy-five strong, flutes, clarinets, bass fiddle, and brass! I gave them the downbeat and they started to play "When the Saints Come Marching In," and in their enthusiasm, the brass nearly blew me off the podium. I wanted them to play much more softly, but I let them play through the first chorus with great gusto and then I said, "That's wunnerful!" or words to that effect—"but how about letting these pretty little girls down here in the front with the flutes and clarinets be heard? Let's feature them to start with." The flutes took over the melody and played so sweetly, so quietly, and yet with such power, I felt a shiver go down my backbone. I brought the clarinets and other reed instruments in next, and finally waved the brass in, and the whole band played to a full crescendo for a rousing finish. We went through it again, and by the end of about a half hour, I felt we had achieved a better balance with more color.

Later that afternoon we presented a public band concert in the Chester Fritz Auditorium of the University, and I was almost as proud of my North Dakota "kids," when we played our newly orchestrated version of "Saints," as I've ever been of my television kids.

It had been a highly informative day. I just hoped I had taught those university students something useful, because they had certainly taught me how quickly you can learn when you want to—especially if you're young! That's long been a pet theory of mine anyway, that the younger you can teach someone any kind of skill, the better. I love to help young people. Next to music, it's the single most compelling joy of my life. I thought a lot about it as I flew back from North Dakota home to California. I decided that one of my principal projects for the future would be to help as many young people as possible reach their full potential, not only for their own satisfaction and strength, but for the strength of the country as well. Maybe, together, we could help re-introduce the idea of developing your own resources, without relying on somebody else to do it for you. That's the spirit that built this country. It's what built our orchestra and a hundred other groups like ours. And it's what will build this country again.

17

My Family Grows Up

THE YEAR SLIPPED by so quickly, I could scarcely believe it was time to go to Tahoe again. Jack worked out a wonderful new show for us, along with Jim and George. I listened and offered advice from time to time, but the three of them had done everything so expertly, I really didn't have to say too much. Mostly, I just watched rehearsals and complimented everyone.

Just before we went up to Tahoe, we held a final rehearsal at the Palladium in Hollywood. It was a very hot day, so we left the big double doors at the rear of the ballroom wide open to let in a little air. That also let out a little band music which you could hear out on the parking lot.

Inside, Jack had set up two work tables, one for Lois and George Thow and their typewriters, and the other for Jim and George and me. But as usual, none of the three of us could sit still and we were up and down the stage steps, dozens of times. We had a little competition during the rehearsal, because Jim had just finished editing the film we had shot on location in Escondido for a special, and the kids kept rushing over to take a quick look at themselves on the monitor between numbers. I peeked, too, and was pleased with what I saw. Shooting any show on location is a tremendous undertaking. This one had come off so well we were all happy.

On stage, the rehearsal moved flawlessly. Ralna and Guy sang their two numbers with their usual style, Ralna looking like a glamorous leading lady in slacks, white silk shirt, and a big floppy straw hat, like Greta Garbo. "What are you wearing a hat in here for?" I wanted to know.

Our glamorous star grinned. "Hiding my curlers," she confessed.

The other girls were dressed more casually . . . Cissy in stretch slacks and one of those midriff tops, as she and Bobby practiced in one corner, and the other girls wearing summery cotton outfits. They looked more like college students than professional entertainers.

Bob McClure, who had flown down from Tahoe to scout the show and see if it offered any production problems for the stage at Harrah's, nodded approval as he watched proceedings. "Just can't see a thing wrong with this one, Lawrence," he said. "Looks like you've got a real winner." Then he grinned. "But where's the flag?"

I laughed. For years I'd had a running gag argument with Bob Ring, vice-president of Harrah's, over the flag we often used at the close of our production numbers. He used to accuse me of bringing up a bigger flag every year. One time I pretended to be very hurt by his teasing, so I said, "Well, Bob, you don't have to worry about it this year. We're not using a flag at all."

"Oh now, Lawrence," he said, a little alarmed. "Listen, I didn't mean for you to take me seriously. Really, I think it's very becoming."

"No, no," I said, trying to look wounded, "no flag this year. You talked me out of it."

That night at the opening performance, Bob and his wife, Lucille, sat in the VIP booth in the center of the room where they had an unparalleled view of the stage. They watched closely as the show moved to its climax when the whole cast came out dressed resplendently in red, white, and blue costumes to sing the "Battle Hymn of the Republic." It was really very impressive and I could see that Bob was very moved. Suddenly, however, his face began to change, and I knew what was happening. Behind me, from the flies overhead at the back of the stage, the crew was beginning to unroll *A Flag*. Slowly, very slowly, it descended until it had filled every square inch of space from top to bottom, and from wing to wing—it looked like the biggest flag in the whole United States of America! In the audience, Bob's jaw dropped lower and lower as he viewed this overwhelming sight, and the moment the show was over he grabbed me. "Welk, you sinner!" he shouted. "I nearly strangled trying to keep from laughing when I saw the size of that flag. Where'd you get it anyway, that's big enough for the state of Texas!"

Bob McClure and I laughed, recalling that incident. "We have a flag again this year," I told him. "But you'll just have to wait and see how big it is." (It was big!)

The mood of happiness persisted all during rehearsal at the Palladium that afternoon, and George seemed particularly happy. He had suffered a grievous personal loss a few months previously with the passing of his lovely wife, Ruth, to whom he had been married for twenty-five years, and we were all worried about him in the weeks that followed. In an effort to lift him out of his depression, I worked out a little scheme. I invited him out to the house one night and told him I was very concerned over my Musical Family and wanted to be sure someone would always be on hand to take over as conductor in case I couldn't be there to do it. "I just don't feel I can handle it all alone any more," I went on, "so . . . do you think you could help me with my chores? Would you help me conduct?"

For the first time in weeks, George's eyes began to sparkle, "Lawrence, I'd like that," he said positively. "I'd like that very much. I've . . . I've missed conducting." I could understand that. George had had his own orchestra for several years before he came with us, and I knew from the way he worked with the boys in our recording sessions just what a fine conductor he was.

"Well, that makes me very happy, George," I said. "We'll start right away."

I didn't say a word about this to anyone, but during the next two days Sam, Don, Ted Lennon, and Jim each called to tell me about the wonderful difference in George. "He's happier than I've seen him in weeks," marveled Jim. "It's as if he had a new lease on life."

I was delighted. I was also tickled to discover that George's new job revealed him as a deep-eyed, first class ham. He truly loved getting out on stage and performing, and watching him at the Palladium that afternoon as he finished up the rehearsal with a wide, sweeping bow, both Jim and I laughed and applauded loudly. George made another hammy bow. "Thank you," he beamed, "thank you. You're a very discerning audience."

At Tahoe, things continued to go well. Jim flew up to help with the staging, and his calm good-humor kept everything running beautifully. He strolled around during rehearsals with a low-voiced suggestion here, a quip there, an encouraging smile here, pulling everything together in his usual expert style. But he really didn't have to do much, because everyone's attitude was just so wonderful. All the kids were thoroughly rehearsed, but all of them seemed anxious to rehearse one more time, make things just a little more perfect. It was so different from the mood of complacency that had infected us the year before, it was almost unbelievable. In fact, things were going so smoothly I was almost worried.

But opening night, in spite of the usual combination of excitement, fatigue, frazzled nerves and elation, turned out to be one of the best we'd ever had. Ralna and Guy made a hit with their number, and Ralna repeated her show-stopping version of "How Great Thou Art." Audiences seem never to tire of that song. And they liked Bobby and Cissy's dance routine, and the specialty number in which they were joined by Mary Lou and Jack Imel. They liked Gail and Dick Dale's Hawaiian song and Anacani's Spanish number and Joe Feeney's Irish version of "Sunrise, Sunset." And they enjoyed the bits of comedy that began to surface in each show, too. When Myron Floren came out in leather shorts and Austrian "lederhosen," for example, to play an accordion solo one night, I remarked on his "wonderful knees." The audience picked up on it right away, so we began to expand "Myron and his knees" into more of a comedy routine. In the same way, when I came out on stage and began remonstrating with the girls over their wild version of "Smoke Gets in Your Eyes," the audience seemed to enjoy that, too, because the more I argued with the girls, the stronger and jazzier the musical beat became—and the more I began to enjoy it! The act ended with me doing a wilder, more energetic dance than they were. As with the "wig bit" and Jack's "old man" routine, we immediately began to experiment with both numbers, trying to find new ways to improve them.

But it was the music, the big-band sound itself, that they seemed to like best of all, and their instant and overwhelming applause after every number spurred the boys into playing better than I'd ever heard them.

I think we loved doing that show, really enjoyed it. Every night I prowled around backstage all during the performance, loving the deep thrilling sounds George was getting from the band, getting cold chills every time Henry Cuesta played "A Closer Walk

With Thee." And I loved being on stage myself. In fact, waiting for my first-act entrance one night as the kids sang my introductory song, I realized how anxious I was to get out there. It was really hard for me to hold myself back. I felt like an old fire horse responding to the bell. The minute I heard that music, I wanted to get out there and perform!

During the day, we all relaxed in the wonderful, crisp air, and each of us turned up sunburned at least once, from the swimming or boating or hiking. Fern also enjoyed herself at the indoor sports available. Every day she'd set out, dressed impeccably as if she were going to a ladies' board meeting-luncheon, and then she'd head for the slot machines. Since she also continued to win almost every day, I kept very quiet. Mr. Harrah entertained all of us once again at one of his fabulous sit-down dinners, where every place card, every place setting, every floral centerpiece at every table had been personally selected by him. And I played golf daily, to my heart's content, took long, wonderful naps in the afternoon, dozing off to the sound of water lapping against the shore of the lake just beneath our bedroom window.

Midway during the run, Lon flew in from Nashville. I was very glad to have my old friend visit for a few days. He had been with us through one of the most momentous years of our lives, and helped so much to get us going again that I knew I would always be grateful to him.

"Oh, now, I didn't do anything, Mr. Welk!" he protested, getting a little pink when I mentioned this to him. "Nothing at all, sir. You and your people . . . and your fans . . . they're the ones who did it."

But nobody knew better than I how much Lon had done for us, and how hard he always worked in our behalf, and I was determined that he take a real vacation for himself while he was with us. I had him stay at the house with us, insisted he take naps, hovered over him like a mother hen, just the way he does with me on the road. We went golfing every day, too, and even though Lon never got much of a chance to play regularly, he is such a natural athlete he beat me consistently. One day when we were zooming over the course in a golf cart, I made a sharp turn, and Lon lost his balance and tumbled out of the cart. Horrified, I jumped out after him, but after I was assured he was all right, I said, "Okay, Lon, watch yourself. You see what happens to people around here when they play better than I do!" Nevertheless, he went right on beating me from time to time.

He came down to the theater every night with me, too, and either stood in the wings or at the back of the house, where he could get a better idea of any problems which might be involved in staging the show on the road. "You've got a great production, Mr. Welk," he said one night. "I've never seen a show with more heart." I felt the same way. I had been feeling for months that we had made tremendous progress in our personal growth since the time we had almost lost the show for ourselves; and one night, close to the end of the run, at a time when our spirits might have ordinarily flagged a bit, or some of the enthusiasm might have gone out of our performance, I realized just how far we really had come. I was standing in the wings, waiting impatiently for my entrance. Out on stage I could see George looking dramatic with his silvery hair and beard shining in the overhead spots, his hands in the air, ready for the overture. I looked around at all the other faces that are so dear to me—at big Barney Liddell, still fighting the battle of the bulge . . . (but still fighting, I thought affectionately!). At Johnny Zell and Mickey McMahon playing so faultlessly. At Bob Ralston, commanding the spotlight as he played a superb solo; at Jack Imel beaming as if he hadn't a care in the world; at Henry Cuesta, performing with such virtuosity I was helpless with admiration.

Then I turned to peer through the side curtain as the kids made their entrance. That year, instead of the usual on-stage entry, they came in through the back of the theater itself, threading their way down through the tables toward the stage, shaking hands with everyone along the way, smiling, singing, laughing. The girls were wearing yellow and orange flowered chiffon dresses, the boys yellow and white flannels, and my heart swelled with pride as they moved through the crowd singing, "We Can Make Music"! They looked so fresh, so clean, so wholesome, so radiant as the spotlights caught them, that I loved every one of them. They were greeting everyone they could, reaching across tables to shake hands with young people, old people, patting youngsters on the head, hugging grandmothers, grandfathers, loving, communicating, entertaining with everything that was in them. Heads turned in the audience as they moved along, happy smiles followed them like ripples in the wake of a boat. They were doing a wonderful, a flawless job of entertaining.

And suddenly I realized, with a start, they had done this all on their own. Not one of them had needed any urging, any coaxing, any supervision on my part at all. And I thought, "Well . . . I guess I've done it. I've finally raised a family that can take care of itself. When I lay down my baton . . . they'll be able to carry on without me."

The thought made me very happy.

But then I saw the kids bounce up onto the stage and heard them sing my introduction:

> ". . . and here he is,
> Mr. Music Maker! . . ."

. . . and I walked out into that familiar blaze of lights and love. And I saw again the warm smiles on the faces of my kids, and felt the warm breeze of love from the audience that I have felt from audiences all over this wonderful, wonderful country . . . and, I must confess . . . I felt even happier!

I guess I won't lay down that baton for a while yet.

Epilogue
"My Musical Family"

As I WRITE these words, my Musical Family and I are still together, still working with the wonderful closeness and dedication which spell the difference between success and failure. We have made several more tours around the country, and almost everywhere we go, our loyal fans still say to us: "Mr. Welk . . . are the people on your show as happy as they appear to be? Or is it all part of an act?"

I would like to answer that question for you now. As you know—if you've read this far in my book—we have had a few tense, unhappy moments. We're human and we have our troubles just like anyone else. But for the most part we have worked together with such joy, I believe I can say that every member of our Musical Family, including me, is a truly happy person. That's partly because we're doing work we love. And partly because we have discovered a way to live up to our highest potential.

I didn't realize this until about six years ago during a performance at Harrah's in Tahoe. I was standing in the wings one night, watching the kids going through their paces, and I was struck with their radiance, their obvious happiness as they performed. I congratulated myself on having rounded up such a group of superior people. Driving home after the show that night I kept on thinking about it. "How in the world," I asked myself, "did a poor farmer like me ever manage to develop such a wonderful musical organization, find such truly wonderful people? What is it that makes them work together with such goodwill, such a high degree of perfection?

I tried to find the reason, and suddenly there flashed into my mind a picture of myself, some forty years earlier, when I first left the farm. Nobody in the world could have been any greener than I was! I was so shy and backward that unless I was actually playing my accordion and thinking about music, it was just agony for me to go out and face a person or an audience. It was at that point in my life I had the extreme good fortune of meeting a man named George T. Kelly, who hired me to perform in his theatrical troupe, The Peerless Entertainers. It was the luckiest thing that ever happened to me, because George T. Kelly changed my life. In an even broader sense, he changed the lives of hundreds of other people, too, because he is actually the founder of the wonderful concept on which we base the system we have used in our musical organization for so many, many years.

His principles, his "rules," were so simple and unobtrusive . . . so basic . . . that I wasn't even aware of them at first. But they were powerful. George changed my life by first treating me as if I were an individual, fully worthy of his time and attention. Then by constantly encouraging me to do better . . . and complimenting me when I did. By setting goals just a little beyond my capabilities, and making me believe I could attain them. (And, with his help, I frequently did.) By drawing me ever closer into his circle of operations so that, almost without realizing it, I was working on a full-time basis with him. And finally, by sharing his profits with me.

This did several things. First of all, it made me feel much better about myself, giving me the self-confidence and feeling of self-worth I needed so badly. For the first time in my life, I felt as if I really were somebody. It made me a much happier person, realizing that somebody else was actually recognizing the hopes that burned so fiercely within my heart, and was trying to help me attain them. (It also sparked in me an overwhelming resolve to help Mr. Kelly attain his.) And it fattened my wallet by giving me a share of the profits. And as poor as I'd been for so many years, that didn't hurt my feelings a bit!

Just being with Mr. Kelly was an education in itself. I couldn't speak much English when I first joined him, and what little I did say came out the wrong way in an extremely thick German accent, of which I wasn't very proud. So he and his wife, Alma, taught me English grammar. George also taught me all he knew about show business, traveling, booking, and how to get along with all kinds of people. That alone, was worth everything. And most important of all, he taught me there are no limits to dreams or achievements. He made me feel nothing was beyond me, and he gave me the kind of unquenchable hope that has lasted all these years. George T. Kelly was a decent, honorable, fair-minded man who shared his life, his experience, and his dreams with me and gave me a model to build my life on. That's exactly what I've been trying to do in our organization. When we take youngsters into our Musical Family we "adopt" them, so to speak, just as Mr. Kelly did with me. When we make them "members of the family" with all the rights and privileges thereof, we do everything we can to guide and direct them, advise and console, inspire and love them . . . just as he did with me.

This plan . . . this system . . . (which we have called at various times our Youth Opportunity Plan or our Family Plan) . . . has been refined over the years, and now operates for us on three distinct levels.

First, is our Vocational Training. When our new people come into the "family" they begin working right away under the expert guidance of Jim Hobson,

George Cates, Jack Imel, Myron, the arrangers, etc., receiving the best possible professional instruction. They also receive invaluable training simply by working with the other singers and musicians in the group, and appearing in the show every week. In our profession, there is no better teacher than actually performing in front of a live audience. Our plan gives our newcomers this chance.

Second, is our Personality and Character Training, a much more subtle, but equally powerful kind of instruction. When our new members see Myron Floren, for example, come into the studio every week, a half hour early, completely rehearsed and ready, calm, smiling, with a friendly word for everyone; when they see Norma Zimmer arrive, flawlessly groomed and also completely prepared, eager to lend a helping hand; when they see Bobby Burgess and Cissy King turn up week after week with a brand-new, finely perfected dance routine which has obviously required hours of preparation; when they see that the inevitable delays and goof-ups which occur in any production fail to make a dent in the good humor and professionalism of our group—then it has a very powerful effect on them. Just by constantly associating with such outstanding people, they themselves learn to be more stable, more self-reliant and dependable, more generous with their own time and talents. They learn to become better and more dedicated persons in every way. Our older members take their obligation to train the younger ones very seriously. It is a matter of pride with all of us, a sort of heritage that we pass on right down the line. Over and over again, I feel it is the same sort of spirit you find in a good family. I'm the "Boss," the father. Jim and George and the other members of our management team are the older brothers and sisters. The younger ones are the children, and we seem to work together just as a family does, to reach our goals.

Actually, what we are doing is sharing our experience, our knowledge, our companionship and our dreams, just as Mr. Kelly did with me.

We complete our sharing by sharing profits, and awarding extra bonuses for outstanding performance in a job. Sharing profits has always been a good way to stimulate a high degree of cooperation, of course, but I believe our system of giving additional unexpected "rewards" is even more inspiring, because we do it in a very personal way. We try always to choose something especially meaningful for the recipient or his family—perhaps a color TV set, or a payment on a mortgage, or a college scholarship. Whatever it is, it says, "We are thinking of you, and what you want." It's this personal, one-to-one relationship which is a key factor in the success of our sharing concept.

These three basic points: Vocational Training on the job; Personality and Character Development; Sharing (of ourselves as well as our profits), form the cornerstone of our growth plan. And holding it all together—is love.

This is especially important in the case of our young people. Why do I say especially important? Because, particularly today, they are the ones so desperately in need of someone to care for them, someone to show them love. Ever since so many families have been brought down to such a low level in our society, our children have suffered. Without the family, I feel so strongly that there is little chance to develop a stable humanity. So perhaps a concerned employer, treating his employees with real consideration—sharing with them, helping them realize their talents—can fill that gap, and give our young people the love they must have in order to develop properly.

But even for youngsters who have already had

the benefit of a fine home life, this plan offers tremendous opportunities for personal growth. I have only to look at the lovely girls in our group to see how greatly they have blossomed and bloomed. It makes me very happy to feel that we have contributed to the growth and happiness of the young men and women in our "family." But at the same time, I realize with great humbleness, what great joy and rich happiness they have given back to me.

Because . . . may I tell you something? Whenever you share something—it increases. That seems to be a law of nature as well as business. The Bible tells us: "Give and it shall be given unto you" and that has certainly proved true in my own experience. We are in better shape today than we've ever been, after years of sharing with our people. And the fact that we are still operating successfully in the very unstable world of music, when practically all the other bands in the business have fallen by the wayside, speaks for itself. Our books speak for themselves. From a purely financial point of view then, our system offers tremendous potential for substantial growth in any kind of business.

But the rewards are far greater than that. This system of voluntary sharing can pull this nation together and give us a new look at life like nothing else can. It can teach our young people what the American economic system is really all about, how it was developed, why it is the best system yet discovered. It can help our young people . . . it can help *all* of us . . . learn to love America again. And I, for one, think it's time we stopped hating the system and the country that is feeding the world. Most important of all, it can develop the kind of strong citizens . . . leaders . . . who can stop the sicknesses spreading in our society, and bring this nation back to health.

We need such leaders, need them desperately. We need fine examples to emulate. I can still remember a traveling accordionist named Tom Gutenberg, who came through Strasburg when I was a young boy, and played a series of concerts in town. He was so good—such a brilliant performer—that he not only sparked me into becoming a better musician, he inspired dozens of other farmers for miles around into learning how to play a musical instrument for the first time in their lives. That one man, with his example of perfection and accomplishment, probably did more than anyone else to further the cause of music and self-development in our small community. If one man, in one small town, could affect so many lives so strongly—think what television can do! This powerful means of communication is already a tremendous source of entertainment and amusement, but it could be so much more. It could inform and educate, inspire and uplift, and present our young people with the kind of "heroes" who can help them learn how to recognize and respond to the best things in life. We should be finding and building this type of leader in all other phases of business and industry, too, because every part of our society contributes to the growth of our nation. We can best improve it by giving our young people a better chance . . . and I believe our Family Plan can help us do it.

You may be saying to yourself, "Oh, my—there he goes again! There goes Welk off on another idealistic dream!"

You're right. I *do* have this dream, and I do think our system of working together and sharing together is an almost perfect way to help achieve these goals. But our Plan is not idealistic in the sense that it is impractical, or cannot work in the rough and tumble market of everyday living. It can and does work right now, as we are proving daily in our organization. But a few basic changes—on a nation-wide level—would allow it to work even better.

1. Establish a more realistic wage scale. This would permit employers to train and develop millions more youngsters in all kinds of businesses and professions.

2. Remove some of the government and union controls. This would cut the paralyzing red tape that now prevents thousands of talented youngsters from getting an early start on a lifetime career.

3. Put God back in our schools. Our coins, our national motto, all say: "In God We Trust." All right then, let's do it! . . . and give our young people the greatest gift of all.

If we could effect these changes, and trust in God—we could change the world.

For one thing, we would unleash so much fresh ambition and enterprise and positive thinking, we could change our moral climate completely, and I think we've lived long enough under clouds of immorality. I hardly need to go into the long list of abuses in the world today. Just pick up your daily paper! The only reason we've been able to absorb such excesses of behavior in our society, is because we still have a good, solid, decent inner core of strength in this country. The overwhelming majority of Americans are still wonderful folks, as I've discovered during my tours. They still believe in God and in our country. They want to save it—and I believe our family system can help do it.

As I say, I didn't even realize we had such a workable plan until I began to analyze why there was such a feeling of contentment in our group. At first I thought it was simply because we were doing work we love, and I have long known that work itself is one of the simplest, best ways to achieve inner happiness. But . . . when you can perform that work in an atmosphere of mutual trust and encouragement, aware that you can rise just as far as your own initiative and talents impel, knowing that the better you do your job, the greater the rewards for you and those around you . . . then you have an almost foolproof way for employer and employee to work together in real harmony. To my mind, our system is the most effective way yet discovered to apply the principles of true social justice.

In my heart, I am convinced that this is because our system is rooted in God's laws, on those principles which founded our nation and first nurtured it into greatness. I believe we must now have a rebirth of those spiritual values, because history has shown us over and over again that no nation, which ignores God's laws can long survive.

Those laws are eternal and unchanging, and the older I grow the more I realize how valid they are, standing as a beacon of truth lighting our way down through the ages. The old rules are still the best rules, because they have stood the test of time. And the best rule of all is still the Golden Rule.

That's why our Plan works! That's why we have such a happy glow on our faces. Because we have recognized that, underlying every other need in life—the need for food, for warmth, for human love, for a dream to follow—is the most pressing need of all: The need for God.

My Musical Family and I believe we have found a way to answer that need. And we invite you to come along with us.

EMCEE MONTY HALL

An autobiography by
Monty Hall and Bill Libby

In his own words, here is Monty's story — a revealing portrait of a multifaceted man and his struggle to make it in the competitive world of show business. What emerges is not only a frank, often painful account of a remarkable career, but a fascinating behind-the-scenes look at the television industry.

"THE STORY OF AN EXTREMELY AMBITIOUS HUSTLER FROM A POOR CANADIAN-JEWISH BACKGROUND AND HIS STRUGGLE TO MAKE IT . . . TOLD WITH A LOT OF INTERESTING, BRUTAL INSIDE-TV STUFF . . . GUTSY!" — *New York Magazine*

"HALL'S LIFE AND CAREER CONTAIN ENOUGH DRAMA TO MAKE EXCITING READING!" — *Variety*

"EXTRAORDINARY." — *Hollywood Reporter*

$1.50

▼ Available at your local bookstore or mail the coupon below ▼